We're never OUT for meals!...and I love it!

Comes meal-getting time I shop right in my Crosley Frostmaster—my choice of many varieties of nutritious, easy-to-prepare, always-in-season frozen foods. More than 100 pounds: frozen meats, fish, poultry, fruits and vegetables for exciting, well-balanced menus. Marketing? Only once in two weeks.

Unexpected guests? Let 'em come! Bad weather? I don't care—I don't have to face it. Yes, we eat better, feel better, save money and food! I love it!

Made by the makers of the famous Crosley Shelvador*; powered by the economical Crosley Electrosaver unit—warranted for five years.

CROSLEY FROSTMASTER

most compact low-priced frozen food cabinet on the market!

Now you can take full advantage of all the savings and conveniences offered by frozen foods, and protect your family against food shortages. Left-overs keep indefinitely, taste better later. Freeze family quantities of pastries, properly processed meats and vegetables . . . they're ready for immediate use when you want them.

The compact CROSLEY FROSTMASTER fits any kitchen . . . gives you extra table-top working surface . . . operates for only a few pennies a week.

CROSLEY FROSTMASTER is the fastest-selling frozen food cabinet on the market today because it's the biggest value! Treat your family to better eating . . . treat yourself to easier meal preparation . . . see the Crosley Frostmaster at your nearest Crosley dealer's, today!

*®TRADEMARK REG.
U. S. PAT. OFF.

CROSLEY

Division—AVCO Manufacturing Corporation
Cincinnati 25, Ohio

© 1948 CROSLEY DIV.
AVCO MFG. CORP.

The Farmer's Wife Slow Cooker Cookbook

101 BLUE-RIBBON RECIPES ADAPTED FROM FARM FAVORITES!

LELA NARGI, EDITOR

Voyageur Press

First published in 2009 by MBI Publishing Company and Voyageur Press, an imprint of MBI Publishing Company, 400 First Avenue North, Suite 300, Minneapolis, MN 55401 USA

Voyageur Press titles are also available at discounts in bulk quantity for industrial or sales-promotional use. For details write to Special Sales Manager at MBI Publishing Company, 400 First Avenue North, Suite 300, Minneapolis, MN 55401 USA.

To find out more about our books, visit us online at www.voyageurpress.com.

Library of Congress Cataloging-in-Publication Data

The farmer's wife slow cooker cookbook : 101 blue-ribbon recipes adapted from farm favorites! / Lela Nargi, editor. — 1st ed.
        p. cm.
   ISBN 978-0-7603-3514-7 (comb-plc)

1. Electric cookery, Slow. 2. Cookery, American. I. Nargi, Lela. II. Farmer's wife.

   TX827.F37 2009

   641.5'884—dc22
2008042496

On the front cover: Digital adaptation of vintage illustration by Deb Hoeffner

Editor: Amy Glaser
Series Designer: Lois Stanfield
Layout: Helena Shimizu

Printed in China

Contents

Introduction...7

A (Brief) History of the Slow Cooker.................11

How to Use This Book—Read This First! 17

Soups..23

Stews, Casseroles, and Sauces.........................47

Main Dishes 73

Side Dishes..109

Desserts...141

Accompaniments..181

Resources...199

Index...205

Introduction

The *Farmer's Wife* was a monthly magazine published in Minnesota between the years 1893 and 1939. In an era long before the Internet and high-speed travel connected us all, the magazine aimed to offer community among hard-working rural women by providing a forum for their questions and concerns, and assistance with the day-to-day goings-on about the farm—everything from raising chickens and slaughtering hogs, to managing scant funds and dressing the children, to keeping house and running the kitchen.

The farmer's wife did not have a slow cooker, but she would have assuredly wanted one! The magazine was filled with articles extolling the virtues of time-saving devices of every stripe, especially those that would cut down on time spent in the

kitchen, where the farmer's wife labored for so much of each and every day. She may have loved to cook for her family, but she also loved to spend time with them outside the kitchen, and she was always looking for ways to create more free family time.

The farmer's wife also did a great deal of cooking for large numbers of people: during the holidays; for family get-togethers; for community festivities; and perhaps that most important of all events, late summer threshing days, when friends, family, and neighbors came together to help each other separate grain from straw after the wheat harvest, using a communal threshing machine. Hearty meals, cooked in generous quantities and celebrating the spirit of community, were the true bailiwick of the farmer's wife.

Contemporary cooks using a slow cooker for the first time or coming back to it after its metamorphosis from the days of the Crock-Pot will find plenty to recommend its method of cooking. The slow cooker is perfect for preparing stress-free family meals if a small amount of time for their preparation can be set aside first thing in the morning to get the ingredients ready for the pot. It is the champion of dinner parties; a vat of chili, enough to feed a

small army, can be left unattended while host and hostess see to other preparations. It is a near-necessity at holiday time when the oven and stove burners are crammed with desserts and all manner of dishes aboil. It is even a welcome addition to the household for summertime meal making, when heat from the stove or oven is so unwelcome due to the outside swelter. Since

Wonderful New Kitchen Ware of Gleaming White Enamel

the slow cooker hardly raises the temperature of the room, a cook can whip up hearty, delicious fare without collapsing from heat stroke.

Not every recipe devised by *The Farmer's Wife* is appropriate or convenient for transferal to the domain of the slow cooker. In fact, a number of recipes tested for this book were utter fiascoes and were discarded. But casseroles, soups, and pudding-based desserts all appear in abundance on the pages of the magazine and are excellent slow-cooker fare. I've tried to stay true to the original ingredients as much as possible while transitioning these recipes. This is easy-going country food for the most part, except for a few instances in which *The Farmer's Wife* splashed out with exotic ingredients and dishes from foreign lands. Almost all the recipes can be doubled or tripled with ease, either to accommodate large gatherings or to store as leftovers for later meals—exactly the sort of penny-saving foresight *The Farmer's Wife* practiced and appreciated.

As usual with the books in this series, make sure you understand the instructions and the order in which they are to be carried out before you start, and make sure you have all the necessary ingredients at hand and assembled. Then get ready to cook up some more farmland history, even more effortlessly than ever before!

–Lela Nargi

A (Brief) History of the Slow Cooker

The history of the slow cooker is a brief and simple one. Simple, because the origin of today's spiffy slow cooker is the beanpot. And there's not much that's simpler than the lowly bean or the method for cooking it—soak, simmer, and eat.

Beanpots were traditionally squat ceramic vessels that were glazed inside and out. They were designed to do nothing more than hold the beans while they were very slowly cooked for a period of many hours over a fire—often enough over an open fire, out on the range, or suspended in the fireplace. These were the days before canned, precooked beans were readily available on supermarket shelves, and housewives and ranch hands were required to prepare their own. The theory behind slow cooking the beans (as opposed to pressure-cooking them, the exact opposite method in which beans can be made ready to eat in a matter of minutes) is that long, slow simmering in a seasoned liquid will allow their innate bland flavor to take on the flavors of molasses, herbs, onions, garlic, and bacon. Boston Baked Beans are the quintessential example of what the beanpot was capable of producing.

Eventually, some innovator hit upon the idea of designing an electric beanpot. Like its nonelectric counterpart, it was meant to slow-cook the beans, but without the use of fuel, and without the cook having to attend to it. One design, the Beanery, was developed by an ill-fated company called Naxon Utilities. When the company was purchased by The Rival Company in 1970, the Beanery was absorbed into the new corporate structure and might have been forgotten. However, the president of Rival asked his on-staff home economist to experiment with the humble pot, to see what it would yield in addition to beans. What resulted was an entire book of "gourmet" slow-cooked recipes, and the remodeling of the Beanery into the Crock-Pot. Its motto: "Cooks all day while the cook's away."

For years, throughout most of the 1970s, the Crock-Pot was hailed as the savior of the modern woman who no longer cared to be chained to her stove and a life of kitchen-bound drudgery, or to be referred to or thought of as a "housewife," for that matter.

The Crock-Pot would allow her to attend to the joys and demands of her career outside the home, yet still prepare delicious meals for her family, quickly, effortlessly, painlessly. A batch of ingredients went into the Crock-Pot in the morning before work and school. By the time everyone had arrived home at the end of the day, dinner was fully prepared. The only thing left to do was to serve the meal and maybe dish out some ice cream for dessert.

Then suddenly, as quickly as it hit, the craze for the Crock-Pot was over. It was rarely heard from throughout the 1980s and 1990s, except when it turned up, dusty and forlorn, at yard sales. Erstwhile cooks discovered the trend of raw food, gourmet frozen dinners, and (gasp!) take-out. For a while, the newspapers and magazines were full of stories about the lost tradition of the family dinner, families who actually owned no dinner table whatsoever, and, most sadly, the breakdown of the entire nuclear family structure thanks to the loss of its seminal custom: the sit-down family dinner.

During the past several years, as Americans have rediscovered the pleasures of homey pursuits of all kinds, including the preparation of easy, nutritious meals, the Crock-Pot has reemerged. It has often been in the guise of the slow cooker. In some instances, it is an appliance that is downright elegant, with a stainless-steel exterior and digital display for cooking settings. A whole host of slow-cooking receptacles are flooding the market, from round Crock-Pots and tall, thin cookers reminiscent of the original Beanery to 7-quart oval cookers that will cook up dinner for a small army. Slow cooker cookbooks abound, but to

COOKS LESS, SMILES MORE

By Uthai V. Wilcox
July–August 1921

There was a vegetable soup for dinner that has required several hours of preparation and cooking. A delicious roast; potatoes that had been mashed and creamed; cauliflower with a cream dressing; lettuce salad; pineapple that had been bought that morning, sliced, and cut in cubes; nuts that had taken a half-hour for the cracking and picking; mayonnaise that had made a right arm ache with the stirring and the beating; homemade jam; hot biscuit; and hot apple pie with biscuit.

"So do you wish any of the roast?" the husband asked his wife as he carved.

"I don't want any. I don't want any dinner at all. I'm too tired to eat."

"Then why do you go to so much trouble? The children and I would be satisfied with a much simpler meal, you know."

"I guess I know my duty to my family."

Then followed the silence that marks the knowledge of the futility of argument, and the father and the children ate a perfectly cooked meal without comment or enjoyment.

She had worked so hard for her family—so much harder than Mrs. White worked for hers—and her family loved her the less for it. *Her* children never trooped into the kitchen after school as Mrs. White's did. There was a pie, a cake, or a pudding in the oven, and a step across the floor might make it fall. *Her* children never played around her as she cooked, for her cooking had always been too elaborate and complex for such interruptions as childish needs and questions.

She never knew how long she sat there, taking inventory of her soul, but it was a long time, and when she returned to the kitchen there was a smile on her face, a smile that was still there when her family came home. It dimpled her cheeks when her husband praised the extragood meal.

"Your cooking improves all the time," he said, with a look that reflected the love in his wife's face.

This time the smile swept away every wrinkle. She knew that she had never cooked less! She had mixed wisdom with her service.

the chagrin of many who remember without fondness some of the sticky, starchy meals to emerge from the original Crock-Pot, they often rely too heavily on prepackaged ingredients, such as canned cream of mushroom soup and ketchup.

This book aims to look backward as well as forward, referring to the wholesome ingredients of *The Farmer's Wife* to satisfy the needs of contemporary cooks who would return to simple cooking with a dash of elegance. The ingredients are simple, straightforward, and honest. In the spirit of the farmer's wife, you are encouraged to use as much produce from your own garden or local farmers' markets as you can. The results will assuredly surprise and delight you.

of course
ENAMELEDWARE
is my favorite

it is so easy to cook with

and so easy to clean . . . stays beautiful for years

SOUPS

Meal-in-One Vegetable Soup
6 Servings

2 lbs. soup bone
2 tablespoons fat
1 tablespoon salt
¼ teaspoon pepper
2 quarts cold water

1 cup canned tomatoes
1 large onion sliced
½ cup diced carrots
½ cup diced celery
½ cup diced potatoes
½ cup peas

Remove a portion of meat from cracked soup bone and cut into pieces. Heat fat and brown meat in it. Place browned meat, soup bone and seasoning in a porcelain enameled sauce pot and add cold water. Cover and cook until boiling point is reached. Then simmer about 2½ hours, or until meat is tender. Skim off any excess fat. Add vegetables and continue cooking until vegetables are tender.

Yes, easy to cook with . . . easy to clean! That's why modern house-wives vote Porcelain Enameled Utensils their most practical time-saver. And see how this gleaming, sparkling kitchenware dresses up your kitchen! Both stain and acid resistant, you'll be pleased to discover that Porcelain on Steel Enameledware stays beautiful for years!

PORCELAIN ON STEEL
ENAMELEDWARE

ENAMELED UTENSIL MANUFACTURERS COUNCIL, Merchandise Mart, Chicago

How to Use This Book: Read This First!

Not all slow cookers are created equal. Nor are they all of equal size. In determining which slow cooker to use in devising and testing the recipes in this book, I opted first for large and second for reliability. Both criteria were met by the highly rated All Clad 6.5-quart model with ceramic insert. It cooks family-size meals and eliminates hot spots, cool spots, and inaccurate temperature measurements. Obviously, not every cook has this model in his or her kitchen. Be aware that cooking times, additions of liquid, and the amounts of ingredients that can be accommodated will all vary with the slow cooker used. You may find that a recipe in this book that calls for 3 hours of cooking time requires something closer to 4½ in your cooker. That 1 cup of liquid is not enough to soften your beans, or it could be the exact opposite. Get to know your slow cooker. If

it is new to you, find out what its quirks and foibles are and take these into account as you become accustomed to cooking with it.

I discovered as I tested recipes that they generally tended to generate liquid in the slow cooker; the temperatures are low and the slow cooker is covered, so no liquid evaporates. Meat and vegetables give off water and juices as they cook, which only adds to the amount of liquid in the pot. For many recipes, you will need to use less liquid than you are accustomed to when cooking on top of the stove or in the oven. Plan to keep an eye on the pot, though. If there is too little liquid to see the dish through to the end of its cooking time, add 1 tablespoon to ¼ cup at a time.

Another discovery is that vegetables take longer to cook with the slow cooker than with other methods. Be prepared for this, and also be aware that slow cooking can leach out much of a vegetable's vitamin content. Some nutritionists recommend a quick sauté on top of the stove before slow cooking to keep some of the nutrients locked inside the vegetable. If this method is not specifically called for in a recipe in this book, feel free to undertake it, if you desire.

One of the great advantages to the slow cooker is its warm function. When the dish is finished, it can remain in the pot at a consistent temperature until you and your family are ready

to eat it. However, be forewarned: if it is placed for too long on warm, dishes, especially with meat, tend to dry out. If a dish is cooked many hours before you are ready to serve it, you would fare better to take the food out of the slow cooker, refrigerate it, and heat it up on top of the stove when you are ready to serve. It's an extra step, but is one that will abolish disappointment and disinterest in the food you find on your plate.

Soups are hands-down the best meals to make in the slow cooker. They are actually meant to generate liquid and they also improve with sitting—qualities that abolish at least two of the above-mentioned concerns. If you are just learning to use your slow cooker, try the soup recipes first. They are sure to be crowd pleasers! Feel free to experiment with soups. The soup recipes devised by *The Farmer's Wife* were mostly extremely simple ones and used only a few core ingredients. For example, you can easily substitute one vegetable for another when making a cream soup; the farmer's wife certainly would have.

There are some things that should never be cooked in the slow cooker, no matter how accomplished or adventurous the cook. These include chickens with skin on, particularly whole chickens or any other large, bony, and greasy pieces of meat; and red kidney beans from their raw state. In the first instance, you will discover a greasy, unappetizing, and potentially germ-laden mess awaiting you in the slow cooker. Since slow cooking is low-temperature cooking, fat from the skin of a chicken or other animal will gradually melt off into the pot, sit on its surface, and allow bacteria to grow and fester, which is unfortunate, as I originally thought to include this recipe from 1912 as an amusing point of interest:

❧ Sheep's Head Stock and Soup

Wash thoroughly a sheep's head, soak it, and break the bones. Put in the pot with the usual soup vegetables and bunch of sweet herbs. Cover well with boiling water and cook. Add salt and pepper. Do not forget that simmering is necessary when making soup or stock, not fast boiling. Simmer 8 hours then strain. Next day remove all fat and fine stock will remain which, if well flavored and cleared, will make excellent soup. A second boiling of the bones, with the addition of barley and chopped vegetables, makes satisfactory Scotch broth.

In the second instance, red kidney beans contain a high level of a toxin that can only be destroyed through boiling, which is never accomplished in the slow cooker. In fact, the low temperature of the slow cooker can actually increase the amount of the toxin. Precooked and/or canned kidney beans are an obvious exception, but extreme caution should be exercised if you plan to cook these beans in the slow cooker. To use dried kidney beans in the slow cooker, the FDA advises that you first soak them in fresh water for at least five hours, change the water, and boil the beans briskly for at least ten minutes.

Finally, not all recipes in this book require exceptionally long cooking. This does not abolish the usefulness of the slow cooker—far from it! In addition to the advantage of being able to walk away from a cooking meal for a period of hours, the slow cooker can boast these nifty features: it does not generate heat on a hot day (as I write this, it is a sweltering 94 degrees Fahrenheit outside, while inside my kitchen I am testing spoon corn bread in the slow cooker with no discomfort whatsoever); even on cool days, it frees up the oven and stove burner space for the preparation of other dishes. This should make the slow cooker the hands-down favorite tool of the holiday season.

FOR YOUR KITCHEN: Some of the Devices That Are True Economies for the Farm Woman

By Wenonah Stevens Abbott
November 1914

The farm wife owes it to her family as well as to herself to have time to devote to the side of life that brings joy to the home circle. She can obtain this time only through better planning and better equipment of her workshop—the kitchen.

The farm wife needs to cultivate a conscience as to the amount of strength she can afford to expend in the general routine of housework. The failures in properly learning to estimate values in woman's work are the cause of the false economics in kitchen appliances.

To escape from the drudgery of life, the housewife must select the best procurable time- and labor-saving tools, so group them as to be able to use them without waste of motion, and adopt a system that will reduce many of the mechanical tasks to automatic process.

[LN: In 1924 some of these devices would have been:]

The three-burner stove [which] cooks dinner over a quick, safe, economical fire.

The tea wagon [which] saves countless steps to and from the dining table.

A bread maker to take the place of hand-kneading.

And, one of the housewife's truest allies, the fireless cooker, [which] "prevents worry and nerve strain, and saves fuel and food values. It automatically attends to the cooking while the housewife looks after other matters. Even with the cheap models, breakfast may be prepared the previous evening and the cooking of dinner and supper got out of the way before breakfast dishes are washed."

bouillon with
toasted cheese
triangles

green pea soup
with minced
hard cooked egg

cream of tomato
soup with
chopped bacon

cream sausage
chowder with
french fried
dumplings

vegetable soup
with cheese
bread roll

Soups

 Split Pea Soup

January 1912

The Farmer's Wife *made this hearty soup in several ways. If she had a meaty leftover ham bone, she used that to fill out the soup. Otherwise, she diced and fried out salt pork or bacon and added that to flavor the peas. You can also use a smoked pork chop, as suggested by Lynn Alley in her excellent book,* The Gourmet Slow Cooker. *Salt judiciously in all these instances, waiting to taste the finished soup before adding spices.*

1 leftover meaty ham bone or 4-inch salt pork or 4 strips bacon,
    chopped and fried or 1 smoked pork chop
2 c. split peas, rinsed
7 c. cold water
2 carrots, peeled and chopped
2 celery stalks, chopped
1 bay leaf
2 to 4 tbsp. heavy cream to serve
salt and pepper to taste

Add all ingredients but cream, salt, and pepper to slow cooker and set to low. Cook 8 hours. If a pork chop or ham bone is used, discard bone and finely chop the meat and add it back to the soup. Add salt and pepper to taste, and then add cream to taste. If the soup is very thick, add a cup or more of water. Stir and serve with Spoon Corn Bread (recipe on page 131), which can be made in the slow cooker the day before.

A cheerful Housewife assures a Successful Meal

❦ Tomato Soup

August 1910

This is a simple, delicious soup that makes the most of very ripe, late-summer tomatoes. You may add a small carrot along with the onion, as The Farmer's Wife did in the original recipe from 1910; or you can opt for a fresher tomato flavor and leave the carrot out. Beef broth was the liquid of choice in the original recipe, but chicken broth (or even water) better enhances the pungency of the main ingredient. Dill makes a lovely garnish. This recipe can easily be doubled or even tripled to feed a crowd, or to freeze until a midwinter meal requires the remembrance of a little summer sunshine.

1 medium yellow onion, peeled, quartered, and sliced thin
1 small carrot, peeled and minced (optional)
1 tbsp. butter
½ c. chicken broth (or water or beef broth; see above note)
3 large, very ripe beefsteak tomatoes, about ¾ lb. each, washed, cored, and cut into bite-size pieces
1 tbsp. sugar
1 tsp. salt
1 tsp. chopped dill, or more to taste
2 tbsp. heavy cream, or more to taste

Sauté onion (and carrot, if using) in butter over low heat and cook until very soft, stirring occasionally. Deglaze with chicken broth and pour all into slow cooker. Add tomatoes and all their juice, salt, and sugar. Set slow cooker to low and cook 4 hours. Pour soup into blender and purée. Pour the soup through a strainer if you do not like the occasional bit of tomato skin turning up in an otherwise smooth soup. Pour into a pot to reheat when ready to serve. Add dill, stir in cream, and allow the soup to warm but do not boil. Check for seasoning and serve.

❦ Vegetable Soup
August 1910, March 1918

The farmer's wife was, most assuredly, NOT a vegetarian (except against her will in wartime, when meat shortages forced her to find ways to finagle a dinner out of beans, cheese, and eggs). Hence this recipe, which calls for the home cook to brown her vegetables in drippings. You can certainly follow this procedure or you can sweat the vegetables in olive oil before adding to the slow cooker. This recipe is equally good in winter when root vegetables are in abundance, or in late spring when the first carrots and potatoes are emerging. The Farmer's Wife would have added heavy cream to enrich the soup at the end. A more refreshing choice is a squeeze of fresh lemon juice.

2 tbsp. drippings from bacon, or olive oil
1 large yellow onion, chopped
3 garlic cloves, peeled and smashed
8 carrots, chopped
4 stalks celery, chopped
2 yellow-fleshed potatoes, such as Yukon gold
water
salt to taste

6 peppercorns
2 tbsp. flat parsley, washed and coarsely chopped
juice of 1 lemon

Wash the vegetables and chop, first peeling the carrots and potatoes. Sweat the onion in the drippings or oil with a little salt until softened. Add carrots, celery, and garlic and sweat until onion just begins to brown—about 5 minutes more. Add to slow cooker along with the potatoes, salt to taste (about 3 tsp.), peppercorns, and water to just fully cover the ingredients (about 6 c.). Set slow cooker to low and cook 4 hours until vegetables are done. If the broth is not flavorful enough, turn the slow cooker to high, remove lid, and continue to cook for ½ hour to evaporate the water and condense the flavors (if you like, a faster way is to boil the soup in a pot on top of the stove). Add parsley and stir to mix. Squeeze in lemon juice to taste—up to 1 whole lemon—and add seasonings to taste. Serve immediately.

❦ Cream of Potato Soup/Potato Chowder

August 1910, May 1918

The substitution of the whites of two leeks for onions will turn this easy American soup into a classic French vichyssoise (blend the soup after cooking and be sure to add the cream!). The farmer's wife would have approved; such a recipe would surely have enlivened her club luncheons. Or stay with the basics for a humble Sunday supper that sticks to the ribs, especially when served with a loaf of crusty bread and some butter.

6 large potatoes, scrubbed, peeled, and diced
1 large yellow onion, peeled and chopped
1 tbsp. olive oil
4 c. chicken broth
salt and pepper to taste
4 slices of bacon, chopped and fried, to garnish
OR chopped parsley or chives
½ c. heavy cream (optional)

Place the potatoes in the slow cooker. Heat the olive oil in a large skillet over a medium flame and add the onion, stirring until it is soft and beginning to brown. Add the chicken broth and stir to deglaze the bottom of the pan, then add the contents to the slow cooker. Set to low and cook 4 hours. The soup may be served hot with the potatoes left in pieces and a garnishing of bacon or parsley.

Variation: For a smooth soup, you may let the soup cool slightly and purée it in the blender, adding cream and parsley or chives to garnish. Taste for seasoning and add salt and pepper if desired.

CORN SOUP A LA NORMANDIE

1½ cups fresh or canned corn
  1 cup meat broth, or 1 cup water
  and 2 bouillon cubes
2½ cups rich milk

1½ tablespoons Minute Tapioca
1 teaspoon salt
¼ teaspoon sugar
½ teaspoon scraped onion

1½ tablespoons butter

Cook corn in broth 10 minutes; force through sieve. Combine with milk, Minute Tapioca, salt, sugar, and onion in top of double boiler. Place over rapidly boiling water and cook 10 to 12 minutes after water boils again, stirring frequently. Add butter. Garnish with popcorn. Serves 4 to 6. (All measurements are level.)

● No white sauce to mix. Instead, use Minute Tapioca as your thickener—and see how full and rich the flavor is and what a wonderful consistency it has! Try this recipe today.

Try Minute Tapioca Cream (see easy recipe on package) with freshly melted chocolate mints as a sauce.

❦ Corn Chowder

July 1938

This is a great soup to make in the middle of summer when the corn harvest is just in, provided you are quick enough to cook up the corn before it turns starchy; which is to say, the same day it is picked. Luckily, frozen corn is readily available so this soup can be enjoyed regardless of the season.

4 slices bacon
2 small onions, thinly sliced
2 10-oz. packages frozen sweet corn (or fresh equivalent)
4 c. chicken broth
½ tsp. sugar
½ c. heavy cream
plenty of pepper

Chop the bacon and fry it out over a medium flame in a skillet. As it begins to soften, add the onions and cook until it begins to brown. Remove with a slotted spoon and place in the slow cooker, along with the corn, chicken broth, and sugar. Set to low and cook 2 hours. Ladle 2 c. of the soup into a blender, add cream, and purée. Return puréed mixture to the slow cooker and stir to mix. Serve piping hot with plenty of pepper.

The woman who owns one will tell you— Write for booklet "What women say"

❦ Black Bean Soup
January 1912

These days, when we think of black bean soup, most of us tend to think of a Cuban variety, laced with lime juice, cilantro, and coriander. But black beans were a staple for the farmer's wife from the very beginning. She certainly recognized the benefit of a bit of acidity to offset the blandness of the beans (seen here with the use of lemon rind and juice), but otherwise her soup followed along the lines of most of the dishes emanating from her kitchen: not much spice and a few vegetables to add body. You may choose to add some cayenne pepper in the cooking, you can serve it with a side of hot sauce, or you can enjoy this soup "naked" as it is prescribed below.

1 tbsp. butter
1 medium onion, chopped
6 celery stalks, chopped
2 tbsp. mustard
1 lemon
1 pt. black beans, soaked overnight
6 c. chicken broth (or water, for a vegetarian option)
salt and pepper
plain yogurt or sour cream to serve

Cook onion and celery in butter over medium-low heat until soft. Add beans, mustard, rind of lemon, and broth to slow cooker. Set to low and cook 6 to 8 hours until tender. Season with salt, pepper, and the juice of the lemon. Ladle some of the soup into a blender, purée, and return to the slow cooker, mixing thoroughly. Serve with a dollop of plain yogurt or sour cream.

Kitchen Ideas
FROM WEST VIRGINIA

ARE you a kitchen drudge, or a skillful kitchen mechanic, at ease in an efficient workshop?

Winter is a good time to check up on your kitchen. With a busier-than-ever spring ahead, you'll want to save time, steps, and strength. Here are some ideas to help you do it, taken from three kitchens in the new rural electrification building at Jackson's Mill, West Virginia. They were planned by Miss Lenore Sater of the U. S. Department of Agriculture and the Home Service Directors of local utility companies.

A. Imagine how easy it would be to prepare a meal in the L-shaped kitchen at the top of the page. At the right there's the mixing center with supplies and tools in refrigerator and cabinet; then the sink and all of the equipment used around it, with dishes within arm's reach; next the stove beside a cupboard containing serving dishes. From there it's only a step to the dining-room door or kitchen breakfast table. Meal preparation and serving go from right to left (the handiest way for right-handed women) with few steps. Curtains are of harmonizing bands of gingham. Oilcloth roller shades take the place of doors.

B. With kettles and pans hung on a sliding partition you need never stoop to reach to the back of a low cupboard. Handiest place for this is between sink and stove.

C. Everything needed for mixing is here. Baking tins stand upright between plywood partitions. Two large cans (one not shown) hold flour and sugar and swing out. Next to the big can note two small shelves which pull out for convenience. The lower work level is for easier mixing.

D. Dishes should be stored at left of sink, as here. Notice how the U-shaped shelves make it unnecessary to move one stack of dishes to reach another. A special space has been made for platters. Plan shelves to fit your dishes, not the carpenter's ideas.

❦ Cream of Celery Soup
October 1911

The beauty of this recipe and others of its ilk throughout the pages of The Farmer's Wife is its inherent simplicity. How can you go wrong with cream and butter? Please note that it's important to trim the tough strings from the largest celery stalks and discard them; otherwise, they'll turn up in your soup after blending with unpleasant results.

1 bunch celery, washed, trimmed of its tough
     outer strings, and chopped fine
15 peppercorns
1 bay leaf
4 c. salted water or vegetable broth
2 tbsp. butter
salt and pepper to taste
¼ c. heavy cream (or more, to taste)
chopped parsley to serve

Add first 4 ingredients to slow cooker, placing the bay leaf and peppercorns in a muslin spice bag, if desired, for easy removal after cooking. Set slow cooker to low and cook 4 to 5 hours until celery is tender. Remove peppercorns and bay leaf. Allow to cool and run celery and broth through blender. Reheat in a large pot over the stove. When the soup is heated through, season with butter, salt, and pepper; remove from flame; and add cream, stirring to mix. Ladle into bowls and garnish with chopped parsley.

*H*ere are four more varieties of extra simple cream soups that
require little more than the main vegetable itself, a liquid, and
milk or cream to finish. The carrot soup is delicious and refreshing
either hot or cold. The asparagus soup can be enriched with cooked
barley after cooking, as The Farmer's Wife did in March 1939, for
a slightly heartier dish. Feel free to experiment with other vegetables;
almost any will make a nourishing and delectable cream soup.

❧ Cream of Carrot Soup
August 1910

2 lbs. carrots, washed, peeled, and chopped fine
1 medium yellow onion, peeled, chopped fine, and lightly browned in
   1 tbsp. butter
6 c. salted water or broth (vegetable or chicken)
salt and pepper to taste
½ c. heavy cream
chopped parsley or fresh marjoram for garnish

Place the carrots, onion, and water or broth in the slow cooker. Set
to low and cook 4 to 5 hours, until carrots are tender. Allow to cool
slightly, then purée vegetables and broth in a blender. Reheat in a large
pot (if you choose to serve this soup hot; otherwise, refrigerate until
ready to serve), season with salt and pepper to taste. Add cream, but
do not allow soup to boil. To serve, garnish with parsley or marjoram.

❧ Cream of Spinach Soup

May 1911

2 lbs. spinach, thoroughly washed
1½ c. chicken broth
2 tbsp. salted butter
salt and pepper to taste
½ c. heavy cream

Add half the spinach, the broth, and butter to the slow cooker. Set to low and cook 2 hours. Cover. After the spinach begins to wilt, stir in remaining spinach. Stir again after second batch wilts and make sure no leaves are sticking to the sides of the slow cooker. When cooked through, allow to cool slightly then purée in blender in batches. Reheat in a large pot on the stove over medium heat; season with butter, salt, and pepper to taste; and add cream. Do not allow to boil. Serve hot.

Variation: From February 1932, you can make Creamed Spinach in almost the same way. Follow above directions and add ¼ c. chicken broth to the pot. When cooked, remove spinach with a slotted spoon from the slow cooker and place in a heated skillet in which the butter has been melted. Sauté briefly and add heavy cream and a sprinkling of nutmeg just before serving.

EASY WAYS TO SPRUCE UP SPRING MEALS

Tomato Juice
Buttered Carrots*
Mixed Greens Salad
Lemon Snow*
Lamb Shanks*
Mashed Potatoes
Beverage

*Recipes below

YOUR FAVORITE FOODS, TOO, deserve a bright new dress these cheerful spring days. See how easily lemons add a dash of color and sparkling flavor to any spring menu.

APPETIZER—*Tomato Juice*
Any appetizer responds to the wake-up zip of fresh lemon . . . a "must" with tomato and other juices.

MAIN DISH—*Lamb Shanks with Lemon**
For something different in an economy dish try this tempting lamb recipe: insert slivers of garlic in 4 lamb shanks . . . dust with flour, salt, pepper and paprika. Brown slowly in melted fat for 10-15 minutes. Add 1 bay leaf, ½ cup fresh lemon juice, 2 tbs. grated lemon peel and simmer 1½ to 2 hours. Add water if needed.

VEGETABLE—*Buttered Carrots**
Lots of vegetables aren't complete without the tang of lemon. Carrots, for example, are wonderful when you thicken the cooking liquid with flour, add a dash of lemon, a pat of butter and a sprinkling of nutmeg.

DESSERT—*Lemon Snow**
Prepare unflavored gelatine (according to directions) with fresh lemon juice. Just before it sets whip vigorously. Serve with a luscious thin custard sauce. Mmm! And don't overlook lemon as a favorite flavoring for pies, cakes, puddings and other dessert treats.

There's another reason for using lemons liberally—HEALTH. Lemons are a rich source of vitamins C and P, a good source of B_1. They aid digestion, alkalinize. Sunkist's famous Lemon Recipe Book has over 100 recipes. It's free. Write Sunkist, Sec. 4805, Los Angeles, 55, California.

Sunkist Lemons in trademarked tissue wrappers are the finest from 14,500 cooperating California-Arizona citrus growers.

FOR GOOD HEALTH AND GOOD FLAVOR

Sunkist
California Lemons

LET'S FINISH THE JOB—BUY WAR BONDS

❦ Cauliflower Cream Soup

January 1916

1 large head cauliflower, washed and broken into small florets
6 large carrots, washed, peeled, and chopped fine
1 medium yellow onion, peeled, chopped fine, and lightly browned in
    1 tbsp. olive oil
6 c. chicken broth
salt and pepper to taste
1 tbsp. butter
¼ to ½ c. heavy cream, to taste
chopped chives, to garnish

Add vegetables and broth to slow cooker. Set to low and cook 3½ to 4
hours, until the vegetables are softened. Allow to cool slightly, then purée
in blender in batches. Reheat in a large pot on the stove over a medium
flame. Add butter, cream, and salt and pepper to taste. Do not boil.
When hot, ladle into serving bowls and garnish with chopped chives.

❦ Asparagus Soup
April 1911

2 bunches fresh asparagus, washed and hard ends snapped off
4 c. salted water
1 tbsp. butter
salt and pepper to taste
¼ c. milk
½ c. cooked barley, if desired

Chop asparagus fine, leaving tips largely intact. Place in slow cooker with water and set to low. Cook 2 to 3 hours until soft. Remove a few of the tips for garnishing. Place the remainder of the soup, cooled slightly, into the blender and purée. Reheat in a large pot over a medium flame and add butter, salt and pepper to taste, milk, and barley, if desired. Do not allow to boil. Serve hot.

A warm-hearted kitchen

The **Heart** *of* **Good Living**

❧ Clam Chowder
November 1928

6 slices bacon, diced
1 qt. potatoes, peeled and diced
4 medium onions, peeled and diced
4 tbsp. butter
salt and pepper
3 c. fish stock or clam juice
1 qt. clams, removed from shells and their liquor reserved
1 c. milk
1 c. heavy cream

Fry the bacon, place in slow cooker, and fry onion in the drippings.
Add to slow cooker with potatoes, butter, salt and pepper to taste, and
stock. Set slow cooker to low and cook 3 to 4 hours until potatoes
are tender. When potatoes are soft, add clams and their liquor, milk,
and cream. Cook until heated through, about ½ hour to 1 hour. Add
seasonings to taste. Serve hot with crackers on top.

Variation: You can make Down East Fish Chowder, published in the March 1929 issue, by making the following substitutions: 1 lb. salt cod for the clams, soaked overnight in the refrigerator in 3 changes of water and cut into bite-size pieces; and 3 c. fish stock (many good fish stores make their own fish stock every day and sell it in pint or quart containers) or water rather than clam juice. Place all the ingredients except the milk and cream in the slow cooker, set to low, and cook 4 to 6 hours until the fish is tender. Make sure you keep an eye on the liquid and add a bit more water if necessary. When all ingredients are cooked, add milk and cream and heat throughout, about ½ hour (you may also do this on top of the stove if you are in a hurry). Serve hot with soda crackers on top.

the STEW'S done!

FARM JOURNAL KITCHEN

SERVING THE MEALS:
The Table Can be Made Attractive without Causing Extra Work

September 1914

How few country women ever have a chance to eat a comfortable meal! With lives spent in the open, fresh air and with the purest of food at their command—food that people in the cities have to pay fabulous sums to obtain and then find that it is never so fresh nor good as it should be—women in the country too often wear themselves out by lacking the repose they require during the meal hours.

There is a charm in a neatly spread table and an unalloyed satisfaction in serving a delicious meal, but deeper and more lasting than either of these delights is the companionship of a mother with her family about the board. She has more to give to the guests who come to her home than a bountiful meal and she should share all the joys of association with them instead of being exiled to the endless round that is universally known as cooking and serving her generous repasts.

Most truly the farmer's wife sets forth "the fruits of the earth" when she spreads her table for company. Only the well planned meal can be bountifully and daintily served without compelling laborious service. The housekeeper who would partake of all its benefits has thought of every requirement for each meal hours ahead of time.

Stews, Casseroles, and Sauces

Beef Stew with Carrots

A simple Farmer's Wife *classic. If you like a thick stew, dredge the beef in seasoned flour before browning; if thin, omit flour altogether.*

2½ lbs. lean stewing beef cut in 1-inch pieces
1 tbsp. olive oil
flour, if desired
salt and pepper
5 cloves garlic, smashed
5 carrots, peeled and chopped
4 to 5 sprigs fresh thyme
2 c. beef broth or water

Trim beef of fat and brown in olive oil, in batches if necessary, to prevent crowding. Or you can dredge beef in flour seasoned with salt and pepper before browning for a thickened stew. Add garlic for last 2 minutes of browning, then transfer beef and garlic to slow cooker. Drain fat from pan and deglaze with water or broth. Add liquid to slow cooker along with carrots and thyme. Set slow cooker to low and cook 7 to 8 hours until beef is tender but not dry. Serve with buttered noodles.

❦ Casserole of Fowl

October 1929

*The farmer's wife would have used a whole, cut-up chicken for this dish.
You can do the same or use chicken pieces. Skinning before cooking
prevents too much grease from forming at the top of the dish, which
creates an environment where bacteria can thrive at low heat (not to
mention creating a greasy, unappetizing mess). Skinning and trimming off
extra fat is recommended for all slow-cooker recipes.*

3 to 4 lbs. chicken pieces, skinned
3 tbsp. olive oil
salt and pepper
flour for dredging, if desired
1 onion, sliced thin
2 stalks celery, sliced
2 small potatoes, peeled and chopped
6 carrots, peeled and sliced
1 c. water or chicken broth
1 bay leaf
parsley for garnishing

Brown skinless chicken pieces in oil over high flame and sprinkle with salt and pepper. Or, dredge the chicken in seasoned flour then brown. Drain on paper towels and place in slow cooker. Add onion and celery to the browning skillet and cook until soft; add salt and pepper to season. Add to slow cooker. Deglaze pan with water or chicken broth and add to slow cooker along with carrots, potatoes, and bay leaf. Set slow cooker to low and cook 4 to 5 hours. A longer cooking time will result in chicken that is falling off the bone. Add seasonings to taste and serve garnished with chopped parsley.

Variations:

Chicken with Dumplings: To make an even heartier meal of this casserole, the farmer's wife added dumplings. It is a tradition many in the United States now call "Southern," but its origins date back several hundreds of years and span Europe. The technique here is adapted from Lynn Alley's excellent book, *The Gourmet Slow Cooker*.

Sift together 2 c. flour, 1 tbsp. baking powder, and ½ tsp. salt. Add 1 scant c. milk and 3 tbsp. melted butter and mix well. A half-hour before the chicken is cooked, turn up the heat on the slow cooker to high. Drop the dumplings by the teaspoonful into the chicken casserole, cover, and cook 30 minutes until dumplings are cooked through. If you are not a veteran dumpling maker, you may want to test one dumpling by dropping it into boiling salted water. If the dumpling does not hold its shape, add a small amount of flour to the dough.

Casserole de Boeuf: *The Farmer's Wife* mandated this variation of the above casserole stating, "Same as for Fowl, using round steak or stewing beef. Serve with tomato slices seasoned with salt and browned in butter."

Keep Your Kitchen Cool *this* Summer!

Be ready for the hot days that are coming. A cooler kitchen makes your work easier and much more pleasant. Here are carefully selected rewards that will reward you month after month with comfort and convenience for each will do your cooking easier and better. Save money by saving fuel as well as keeping cool. Get the whole set now.

Dutch Oven

Reward No. 629J—A real aluminum Dutch Oven with handy cook's fork and shakers postpaid for two or more orders for The Farmer's Wife Magazine amounting to only $2 . . . Top of the stove cooking with a low fire calls for a Dutch Oven. With a capacity of five quarts, made of solid aluminum, dome cover, cool handles, special tray and satin finish bottom for heating efficiency, every housewife will appreciate this new reward.

Ovenette

Reward No. 566J—Postpaid for two or more orders for The Farmer's Wife Magazine amounting to only $2 . . . Bakes or roasts perfectly on any type of stove with the least possible heat. Bakes as well as your regular oven with a quarter the fuel. Complete with recipes for a comfortable kitchen on hottest days.

Clamp Seal Cooker

Reward No. 502J—Eight quart aluminum Cooker postpaid for two or more orders for The Farmer's Wife Magazine amounting to only $2 . . . During the hot summer months it will be appreciated most. Foods do not shrink when cooked this way, all rich concentrated flavors are retained. This marvelous cooker gives you hours of added time, while you are busy outside, it prepares a whole meal without "pot watching" . . . Larger size to hold quart Mason jars for canning postpaid for three or more orders amounting to only $3—Reward No. 628J.

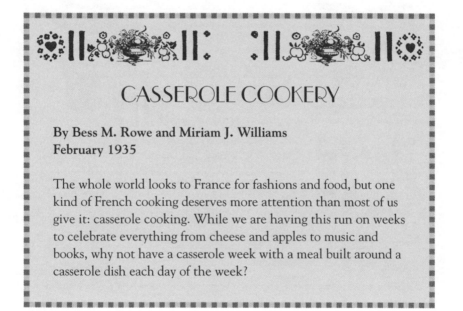

CASSEROLE COOKERY

By Bess M. Rowe and Miriam J. Williams
February 1935

The whole world looks to France for fashions and food, but one kind of French cooking deserves more attention than most of us give it: casserole cooking. While we are having this run on weeks to celebrate everything from cheese and apples to music and books, why not have a casserole week with a meal built around a casserole dish each day of the week?

❧ Brunswick Stew

March 1938

Brunswick County, Virginia, claims to be the region where this dish originated. Legend has it that a local chef out on a hunting expedition in the early nineteenth century stewed some freshly slaughtered squirrels with onions and bread over a campfire for the evening meal. By the time The Farmer's Wife got ahold of the dish in March 1938, squirrel had morphed into chicken and quite a number of vegetables had been added to the mix. You can try out this fancier version, or stick to basics with just the chicken, breadcrumbs, seasoning, and butter to stew in the pot.

1 stewing chicken cut in pieces, skin removed
½ c. breadcrumbs
salt and pepper
2 onions, peeled and sliced
2 tbsp. olive oil
4 potatoes, washed, peeled, and diced
1 pt. lima beans, fresh
8 tomatoes, chopped
corn cut from 8 ears
lump of butter
¾ c. water or broth

Mix the breadcrumbs with seasoning and dip the chicken in it to coat. Heat olive oil in large skillet over medium-high flame. Add chicken and brown on all sides; place in slow cooker. Add onions to skillet and cook until lightly browned; add to slow cooker along with remaining ingredients. Set slow cooker to low and cook 4 to 6 hours until chicken and vegetables are all very tender. Season to taste. Serve hot.

DEEP-DISH
BRUNSWICK STEW

Photo: William Hazzard/Fereghan Studio

❧ Chili con Carne
February 1926, December 1928

To The Farmer's Wife, chili con carne was high exotica. It was a dish from a hot, distant land that incorporated a strange mixture of meat and beans and (gasp!) spice. The Farmer's Wife was nothing if not bland of palate. And curiously, though the dish conjured Mexico and other countries south of the border to the magazine and its readers, food historian Alan Davidson, in his Penguin Companion to Food, points out that it originated in Texas, although it possibly had its roots in the pots and pans of the poor Mexican immigrant community in San Antonio. Still, the dish makes numerous appearances in the pages of the magazine over the years, a testament to the fact that as temperate as her everyday fare may have been, the farmer's wife maintained a hearty curiosity for that which was new to her, especially if it meant the discovery of a meal that drew her away from the realm of kitchen-bound monotony. At any rate, chili con carne would have called for many items already in the farmer's wife's larder: onions, garlic, beef, tomatoes, and beans. Often, however, the recipes in the magazine more closely resembled a simple stew rather than chili. The Farmer's Wife often attempted to define and re-create this alien meal. See the differences in ingredients listed in the two recipes below. Attempts have been made here to follow the more "traditional" of the two recipes as much as possible, making adjustments for contemporary taste buds. It should be noted that not all chili powders are created equal. Some are mild, and some run very hot. Know which kind you are using before you decide how much you will add. In testing the recipe, I used a moderately spicy Indian chili powder, which gave a pleasantly spicy flavor.

2 c. pinto beans, soaked overnight in enough water to cover

2 c. crushed tomatoes

1½ lbs. beef, such as chuck or brisket, trimmed of fat and sliced in ½-inch slices, each then cut in half lengthwise and sliced again to make short, thin slices

2½ tsp. salt (or more, to
    taste)
2 tbsp. sugar or brown
    sugar
1 bay leaf
4 c. water
2 medium onions,
    quartered and thinly
    sliced
2 slices bacon, chopped
1 tbsp. ground cumin
1 tbsp. ground coriander
1 tsp. moderately spicy
    chili powder (more or
    less, to taste)
½ tsp. ground ginger
chopped cilantro, if
    desired, to garnish

Chili con carne pie

BY RUTH BEHNKE Food Editor
Photo: William Hazzard/Faraghan Studio

Drain the beans and
place them in the slow
cooker with the tomatoes,
beef, salt, sugar, bay leaf,
and water. In a medium
skillet fry the bacon with the onions over a medium-low heat until the
onions are soft. Add the spices, stir to mix, and add the mixture to the
slow cooker. Stir to mix, making sure all ingredients are covered with
water. Set slow cooker to low and cook 8 hours. Serve over cooked
rice and garnish with chopped cilantro.

RED BEANS AND HOW TO USE THEM FOR CHILI CON CARNE

By Helena Korte
February 1926

All beans need long, slow cooking. Hastily prepared they are unpalatable and indigestible. The method described here originated with a gentleman of New England stock, well acquainted with the beanpot of his fathers. After going to California, he experimented with the native red beans often called Mexican beans because the Mexicans grow them as a staple article of food and consume them in large quantities. They are locally known also as *frijoles*, which is the Mexican name for this branch of the bean family. When well-cooked these red beans seem richer and to many palates are more agreeable in flavor than the common navy bean.

The materials needed for [chili con carne] are:

2 c. red beans
½ lb. salt pork
2 to 3 ripe tomatoes or 1 c. canned tomatoes
2 large onions
1 large clove garlic
1 tbsp. sugar
1 tsp. ginger
1 tsp. mustard
salt to taste
2 or 3 red chili peppers

continued on next page

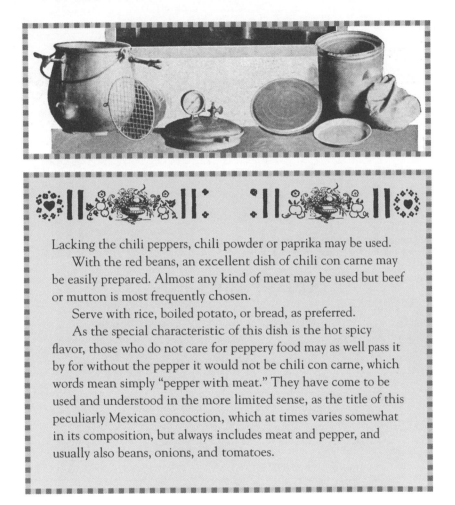

Lacking the chili peppers, chili powder or paprika may be used.

With the red beans, an excellent dish of chili con carne may be easily prepared. Almost any kind of meat may be used but beef or mutton is most frequently chosen.

Serve with rice, boiled potato, or bread, as preferred.

As the special characteristic of this dish is the hot spicy flavor, those who do not care for peppery food may as well pass it by for without the pepper it would not be chili con carne, which words mean simply "pepper with meat." They have come to be used and understood in the more limited sense, as the title of this peculiarly Mexican concoction, which at times varies somewhat in its composition, but always includes meat and pepper, and usually also beans, onions, and tomatoes.

The entertaining we enjoy most, and find easiest to do, starts when we ask a few of our friends to

"*Come to Sunday Supper*"

TAMALE PIE DINNER

October 1920

"Anna, how can you be sitting here mending stockings if you're going to have 12 people to dinner at 6:00? Did you get Hannah to come help?"

"Don't worry, Belle! There isn't a thing to do until 5:00. I did the cooking yesterday afternoon. After our noon dinner I set the table, and so I can rest now and be fresh and calm when my guests come."

This dinner is of Spanish origin, with American variations.

Mexican Kidney Beans: Cooked until soft and seasoned with salt and pepper and a small slice of bacon or pork.

Tamale Pie: 4 lbs. of neck piece of beef, 4 large onions, 6 dried chili peppers, hominy grits, 2 qts. tomatoes, 1 c. raisins, onion salt, garlic salt, paprika, chili powder, and pepper.

❧ Tamale Pie Dinner
October 1920

Here is a reasonable approximation of the above, so-called "Spanish" tamale pie dinner. It is, in fact, wholly American: a somewhat homier version of chili con carne. It eliminates more contemporary additions of sliced black olives and prepared chili sauce but substitutes ground beef for beef neck bone, which is a greasy challenge for the slow cooker.

1 tbsp. olive oil
1 lb. ground chuck
2 medium yellow onions, chopped
3 to 4 cloves garlic, smashed
14-oz. can pinto beans, rinsed and drained
1 tbsp. ground cumin
1 tsp. ground coriander
½ to 1½ tsp. chili powder, to taste
2½ tsp. salt
1 c. cornmeal
1½ c. chicken broth
1½ c. crushed tomatoes
⅓ c. raisins
1 c. sharp cheddar
   cheese, grated

Heat the oil in a large skillet over a medium flame and add the meat and onions. Cook, stirring frequently, until onions are soft and meat has lost its pink sheen. Add all the remaining ingredients except the cheese (or add the cheese to the mix, if you prefer), stir well, and evenly spread into slow cooker. Cover and cook on low for

4 hours, leaving the lid ajar for the last hour to evaporate some of the moisture. If you have not added the cheese to the mixture before cooking, sprinkle it over individual portions before serving.

Variation: Substitute corn kernels for the raisins.

❧ Lentil Stew

February 1922

Lentils were a staple of the farmer's wife's pantry, as was lentil soup, one of the magazine's recipes that was adapted to make this hearty stew—a whole meal in itself. The blandness of the grains and legumes may typically require more salt than you might originally conceive; however, start with a smaller quantity for cooking and season with more as necessary once the cooking is complete. Surprisingly, butter elevates this from humble hominess to a truly delicious repast.

1 c. brown lentils, rinsed
½ c. barley, rinsed
2 large carrots, washed, peeled, and finely chopped
2 stalks celery, washed and finely chopped
1 small onion, finely chopped
5 cloves
1 tsp. salt, or more, to taste
6 c. water
1 lb. spinach, washed and chopped
butter to serve

Place all ingredients except spinach and butter in the slow cooker. Set to low and cook 4 hours. In the last half-hour or hour of cooking, add the spinach and stir. When ready to serve, taste for seasonings, adding more salt and some pepper, as necessary. Ladle into bowls and top each serving with ½ tbsp. butter. Serve with rice, if desired.

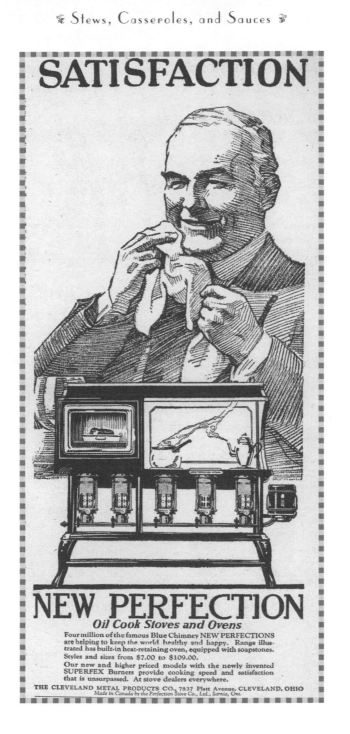

❧ Vegetable Stew

March 1930

In March 1930, the farmer's wife clearly found herself with a surplus of winter-stored root vegetables and canned vegetables and a deficit of ideas for what to serve for dinner. In one article, there were recommendations for four varieties of Vegetable Stew. The combinations are left intact below. You can use any of the recommendations or devise your own.

Version I

½ c. carrot
1 ½ c. potatoes
1 c. lima beans
1 c. peas
¼ c. onion
½ c. tomato
1 tbsp. butter

Version II

2 sweet potatoes
1 small onion
1 ½ c. green beans
1 c. corn
4 okra pods
1 large tomato
salt and pepper

Version III

1 c. potato
1 c. tomatoes
1 onion
½ c. celery
½ c. carrots
½ c. peas
½ c. cabbage

Version IV

½ c. onion
½ c. potato
¼ c. celery
1½ c. tomato
⅓ c. carrot
½ c. chopped okra
butter

Basic instructions for all versions: Wash all vegetables, peel those that need it, and shuck or shell corn, beans, and peas. Chop large vegetables into small pieces. Heat olive oil or bacon drippings in a large skillet and brown onions, carrots, celery, and the like. Add to slow cooker with remaining ingredients and ½ to 1 c. water or stock. Cook 2 to 4 hours until all the vegetables are tender, stirring occasionally and making sure there is ample water at the bottom of the pot. Taste for seasonings and add salt, pepper, lemon juice, and/or any herbs you desire. Serve over rice, noodles, or cornbread.

American Chop Suey

January 1939

The Farmer's Wife *loved Chop Suey. It appeared on the pages of the magazine time and time again over the years, each with a slightly different variation of ingredients and always with the moniker "American." Indeed, this dish is definitively American, despite the inclusion of Asian ingredients like soy sauce, and in this version, water chestnuts, bean sprouts, and peanuts. This is a good way to stretch a small amount of high-quality pork (2 very meaty organic pork chops were used in testing), also an Asian technique, and it cooks up relatively quickly. Long cooking will tenderize tough and rubbery meat. Keep an eye on the liquid, as mushrooms tend to absorb quite a bit. Add an extra tablespoon of broth at a time, if you find the liquid level is low.*

1½ tbsp. olive oil
1 whole bunch celery, sliced very thin
1 small onion, thinly sliced
1 lb. pork, cut into very small cubes
3 cloves garlic
¼ c. chicken broth
2 tbsp. soy sauce
1 tbsp. mirin
½ c. shiitake mushrooms, thinly sliced
1 5-oz. can water chestnuts, sliced
pepper to taste
2 c. bean sprouts
chopped peanuts, to garnish

Heat the oil in a large skillet, add the celery and onions, cook until translucent, and add to the slow cooker. Brown the pork in the skillet with the garlic and add to slow cooker. Deglaze the pan with the chicken broth. Add the broth to the slow cooker along with the soy sauce, mirin, and mushrooms. Cook 2 hours until the pork is very tender. Add water chestnuts to just warm throughout. Season with pepper to taste. Serve, garnishing with bean sprouts and chopped peanuts.

❦ Tomato Sauce

April 1925

Here's a version of spaghetti sauce without the beef, although it's hardly a vegetarian option thanks to the salt pork. The farmer's wife didn't always eat meat with each and every meal. During wartime the magazine was rife with meatless solutions that incorporated grains, eggs, and cheese. You can make the sauce meatless, should you wish to, by merely omitting the pork and browning the vegetables in olive oil. To make this a tad more Italian, substitute 3 cloves of garlic for the cloves.

¼ c. minced salt pork, or 1 to 2 slices of bacon, chopped
½ c. chopped carrot
½ c. chopped celery
1 small chopped onion
1 qt. chopped tomato
1 bay leaf
5 cloves
salt and pepper to taste
parsley to garnish
cooked spaghetti and grated parmesan cheese to serve

Fry out the pork, add to the slow cooker, and lightly brown the vegetables in the drippings. Drain. Add to slow cooker along with tomato and spices. Set to low and cook 2 to 3 hours until the flavors are well incorporated. Season to taste. Serve over spaghetti and top with parmesan cheese.

Main Dishes

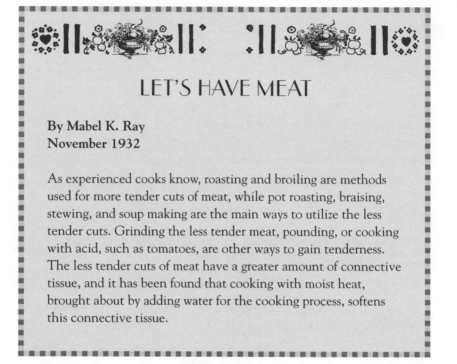

LET'S HAVE MEAT

By Mabel K. Ray
November 1932

As experienced cooks know, roasting and broiling are methods used for more tender cuts of meat, while pot roasting, braising, stewing, and soup making are the main ways to utilize the less tender cuts. Grinding the less tender meat, pounding, or cooking with acid, such as tomatoes, are other ways to gain tenderness. The less tender cuts of meat have a greater amount of connective tissue, and it has been found that cooking with moist heat, brought about by adding water for the cooking process, softens this connective tissue.

❧ Roast Pork and Apples

October 1922

The Farmer's Wife *was big on roasts; they were a convenient way to cook up enough meat for an entire hungry family, and any leftovers had numerous practical purposes—for sandwich filling, breakfast hash, and next-day soups or casseroles. But she did not entirely eschew smaller cuts, like pork chops. This recipe pays homage to her commitment to that famous autumn combination of pork and apples, using pork chops rather than a whole pork loin to allow for easy serving (no carving!). For best results, chop apples and onion to a uniform size.*

6 boneless pork loin chops, cut ¾-inch thick
olive oil
salt and pepper
1 medium onion, peeled and chopped
6 sour apples, peeled, cored, and chopped
4 cloves garlic, peeled and smashed
1 tbsp. brown sugar
¼ c. apple cider
nutmeg

Brown pork chops in a large heavy-bottomed skillet in 1 tbsp. olive oil over high heat and sprinkle with salt and pepper. Place in one layer at bottom of slow cooker. Add 1 tbsp. more olive oil to skillet, add onion, and sprinkle with a little salt and pepper. Sauté onion until soft. Add apples and garlic and sauté an additional 2 minutes. Spoon mixture over pork chops, sprinkle the sugar over the mixture, and pour in cider. Cook 4 to 6 hours on low until tender (the exact time will depend greatly on the quality of meat used). A generous grating of fresh nutmeg just before serving vastly enhances this dish.

I'LL HAVE NO ASHES IN MY KITCHEN EVEN IN WINTER!

❦ Lamb Curry
April 1926

The Farmer's Wife *made curry with a very small amount of the mixed spice, boosting its sauce with a generous dollop of milk. It is not a combination we think much of these days, but for a time it was a very popular Americanization of Indian so-called curries of vegetables or meat cooked with a variety of spices and, often, yogurt. (If you've ever seen the 1940s film* Adam's Rib, *starring Spencer Tracy and Katherine Hepburn, you've witnessed the two main characters in their kitchen whipping up a lamb curry from a leftover roast, some curry powder, and milk on the maid's night off.) The recipe below attempts to concede to both old and new. It calls for prepackaged, nondescript curry powder instead of a more traditionally Indian breakdown of specific spices, but it is also enhanced by*

tomatoes (for some much-needed acidity), raisins (a little sweet to balance the acid), and cilantro, which no respectable Indian kitchen would ever do without. Serve over basmati rice for an even more authentic meal.

2½ lbs. lamb for stew, cut in 1-inch pieces
2 tbsp. olive oil
2 medium onions, chopped
2 cloves garlic, smashed
2 to 3 tsp. curry powder (depending on the heat of the spice and your
    own preference)
8 green cardamom pods
1 tsp. ground cumin
salt
pepper
1 c. chicken broth or water
1 c. crushed tomatoes
½ c. shredded unsweetened coconut
½ c. raisins
chopped fresh cilantro, to garnish
yogurt to serve
cooked rice to serve

Trim the lamb of fat, then brown in a large skillet in the oil over a high flame and sprinkle with a little salt. Remove the meat with a slotted spoon and place in the slow cooker. Drain the skillet of fat, then add onions, garlic, and a little more olive oil, if necessary. Cook until onions are soft and slightly brown. Add curry powder, cardamom, and cumin and stir for several seconds to mix. Add to slow cooker. Deglaze skillet with chicken broth or water, add tomatoes, and stir briefly. Add to slow cooker. Set the slow cooker on low and cook for 4 to 5 hours until very tender. Add the coconut and raisins after 3 hours to preserve their flavor. Serve over rice with a dollop of yogurt and cilantro to garnish.

Variations:
You may substitute beef or chicken for lamb.

Omit the crushed tomatoes for a simpler flavor.

In December 1914, *The Farmer's Wife* also recommended Rabbit Curry. "Europeans frequently substitute rabbit curry or rabbit pie for the Christmas fowl," she instructed. "Clean [and skin] a young rabbit. Cut into pieces as for frying. Fry in bacon fat until a light brown. Fry 3 sour apples and 2 onions, finely chopped. Add 1 tsp. curry powder and soup stock, salt, and pepper to taste." Add all to the slow cooker and follow the instructions above for Lamb Curry. Serve hot over rice or boiled, buttered noodles.

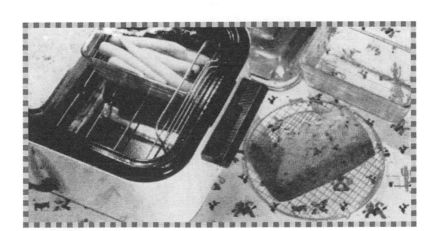

TABLE TALK

By Anna Barrows
February 1916

The tougher muscles such as the neck, shoulder, shank, and flank
are not suitable for broiling or roasting even when separated from
the bones. These cuts are commonly cooked in other ways. But
to develop flavor they are often browned before putting in water.
Therefore, when we cook a large porterhouse steak, it is well
to reserve the flank end for a second serving and add it to the
bones and any portions left. Or we may buy a pound or so of less-
expensive meat to combine in stew with whatever is left of
the steak.

In the same way we may bone lamb or veal chop, all the
bones may be put in cold water with a portion of flank or neck
for a good stew. Stews are not appreciated when the meat is
tough or mushy or otherwise unattractive. Bones, skin, and
surplus fat need to be carefully removed.

Pillsbury's POT-LUCK PIE . . . with a marvelously tender, flaky topping . . . from that *dependable* all-purpose flour, Pillsbury's Best!

❦ Adouba

June 1938

This is a dish of Greek origin where pork is rendered especially savory with spices, vinegar, and long slow cooking.

2 lbs. boneless pork shoulder
1 tbsp. olive oil
dash cayenne
spice bag with:
  1 tsp. whole cloves

1 tsp. whole or ½ tsp. ground
  allspice
2 sticks cinnamon
2-inch piece ginger
¾ c. cider vinegar
1 tsp. salt

Cut pork in squares, trim off fat, and brown in the oil over a high flame. Add to slow cooker with remaining ingredients. Set on low and cook for 4 hours until very tender. Serve with rice.

❧ Swedish Meatballs
May 1928

Here is a classic recipe for the farmer's wife, who often hailed from Scandinavia. This is a highly traditional version of the recipe, and one that was not originally enriched with sour cream when it ran in the magazine. If your taste buds require it, you may choose to add a small amount of sour cream after cooking.

1 lb. lean ground beef
½ lb. lean ground pork
1 medium potato, grated fine
1 egg
¾ c. fine dry breadcrumbs
½ tsp. pepper
1 tsp. salt
½ tsp. sugar
1 small onion, grated
2 to 3 tbsp. milk
3 tbsp. butter
½ c. sour cream, if desired
¼ c. chopped parsley, to garnish
buttered egg noodles or boiled potatoes, to serve

Beat egg well and combine all ingredients, down to the milk. Form into 1-inch balls. Brown in butter. Drain and place in slow cooker. Add 1 c. beef broth. Set slow cooker to low and cook 2 to 3 hours until cooked through but not mushy. Be sure to stir occasionally to ensure that all sides of the meatballs are cooking in the broth so they will not dry out. Remove meatballs with a slotted spoon to a bowl. Taste the broth for seasoning and adding sour cream, if desired. Pour a little or all of the sauce over meatballs and garnish with parsley. Serve over buttered egg noodles or boiled potatoes.

❦ Ground Steak, Italian Style
November 1917

This recipe is for spaghetti and meatballs, plain and simple! Although this dish was certainly not a farmland staple in 1917, several articles in the magazine around this time were devoted to learning the secrets of Italian sauce from real, live Italians! Contemporary cooks will find nothing especially exotic or unusual about this dish, but they may be gratified by the simplicity involved in browning the meatballs and leaving them for a long simmer in the slow cooker. Be sure to stir every now and then to ensure that the tops of the meatballs are covered with sauce so they don't dry out while cooking.

2 lbs. ground sirloin
2 tbsp. olive oil, plus extra for browning the meatballs
¼ c. stale breadcrumbs
1 tsp. salt
pepper to taste
⅛ tsp. grated onion
2 eggs
2 28-oz. cans crushed tomatoes
1 c. water
1 onion
2 cloves garlic, crushed
1 tsp. salt
2 tbsp. butter

Mix first 7 ingredients and form into small meatballs the size of walnuts. Brown in a large skillet in enough olive oil to cover the bottom over a medium-high flame. Turn several times to brown all over. Remove browned meatballs with a slotted spoon and place on a paper towel to drain. While the meatballs are browning, mix all the remaining ingredients in the slow cooker. Add the meatballs once they are drained. Set slow cooker to low and cook 4 hours. Serve "in the center of a platter with macaroni all around and sauce over all."

❧ Real Italian Spaghetti
May 1925

As an alternative to the above recipe, you could try this one for spaghetti with meat sauce. It appeared in the magazine eight years after the recipe for Ground Steak, Italian Style and used cubed beef rather than ground. Here's what The Farmer's Wife *had to say about it:*

"A representative of The Farmer's Wife *had the privilege of visiting a group of Italian women who were studying lessons on child feeding, given by the home economics extension worker from Luzerne County, Pennsylvania, Miss Nitzkowski. An interesting side feature of the meeting was the preparation of real Italian spaghetti by Mrs. Scalza, the woman in whose home the meeting was held. The recipe, given here, serves 12 people." [LN: Only if they are not very hungry!]*

2 lbs. round steak, cut in 1-inch squares
1 tbsp. lard
1 28-oz. can crushed tomatoes
1 medium onion, chopped
salt and pepper to taste
2 lbs. spaghetti, cooked
grated parmesan cheese

Brown the meat in the lard, drain on paper towels, and add to slow cooker. Brown onion. Add to meat along with tomato, salt, pepper, and 1 c. water. Set slow cooker to low and cook 4 to 6 hours until the meat is very tender. Adjust seasonings. Serve over cooked spaghetti and top with parmesan cheese.

❦ "Barbecued" Beef on Toasted Buns

Utah Club Plate Luncheon
Submitted by Mrs. P. H. Rasmussen
October 1939

You probably know them as "sloppy joes," but to the lunching ladies of Utah in 1939, these hot open-face sandwiches were considered elegant club fare. Why they were considered "barbecued" is anyone's guess, but the resulting dish is delicious and pungent, thanks to the use of green rather than red tomatoes, and it's not at all difficult to achieve in the slow cooker. Hamburger buns were surely the bread of choice here, but you may substitute something more contemporary for ladies-who-lunch, such as ciabatta rolls or small challah buns.

⅓ c. olive oil
3 lbs. ground lean beef
1 large yellow onion, peeled and chopped
1 c. celery, washed and chopped
2 c. green tomatoes, chopped fine and all liquid reserved for the
    slow cooker
salt and pepper to taste
buns
butter

In a large skillet, brown beef, onion, and celery in the olive oil over a medium-high flame. Add to the slow cooker with the green tomatoes and their juice and salt and pepper to taste. Set slow cooker to low and cook 2 to 3 hours until the meat is cooked through and the tomatoes have softened into a sauce. Check for seasoning. Split the buns, toast them, spread butter on them, and top with the beef mixture.

■ ■

❧ "Barbecued" Ribs
February 1939

As long as men have been hunting, they have been throwing meat over an open fire to cook it. Barbecue, as food historian Alan Davidson points out, is and always has been a supremely male activity. This explains why The Farmer's Wife *put the name of this recipe in quotes—a woman was assumed to be the cook. She was also going to do the cooking in the oven rather than over a pit of coals or bundle of kindling. In the United States, pork barbecue is a distinctively Southern tradition, although it is one that has been adopted by now across the country. A traditional vinegar-based sauce was whipped up in the original recipe for these ribs with rather an overabundance of ketchup. Below, an only slightly sweet and sticky sauce has been spooned over the ribs for a succulent summer dinnertime treat.*

3 to 4 lbs. spareribs, cut into individual pieces
2 tbsp. butter, melted
¼ c. vinegar
1 tbsp. Worcestershire sauce
1 tbsp. brown sugar
1 tsp. celery salt (or regular salt, if you prefer)
½ tbsp. mustard
2 tbsp. ketchup

In a large skillet, brown the spareribs on all sides over a medium-high flame. Meanwhile, mix up all the remaining ingredients in a bowl. When the ribs are browned on all sides, transfer them to the slow cooker and spoon the sauce over them, turning to coat on all sides. Set the slow cooker to low and cook 3 to 4 hours until the meat is very tender. Turn the ribs now and again to make sure all sides are immersed in the sauce to prevent them from drying out. Serve at once.

The new way to cook is with Karo!

❧ Calabasita y Gallina (Pumpkin and Chicken)
February 1930

The true Spanish name for this classic Tex-Mex dish is Calabasita con Pollo. Who knows how The Farmer's Wife hit upon the title she gave the recipe when it ran in the magazine in February 1930. It was probably an attempted literal translation of the words for "little squash" and "chicken." The original squash used in this dish was cooked up by Mexican settlers in Texas and was thought to be a variety of winter squash called cushaw. It could be picked young and tender and eaten with the skin on, or it could be left longer on the vine to harden into a more pumpkinlike squash to be stored for winter. Many contemporary recipes for Calabasita con Pollo call for the use of zucchini. You can use a winter squash along the lines of a (peeled) Japanese kabocha to delicious effect. Zucchini cooked in the slow cooker tends to simmer down to mush, while the harder winter squashes manage to maintain some of their texture. A little bit of seasoning has been added to this recipe to make up for the always shockingly timid palate of The Farmer's Wife.

2 tbsp. lard or olive oil

I small chicken, chopped and skinned (or use 3½ lbs. skinned
   chicken pieces)

I medium onion, chopped

I tbsp. cumin

I small tender green pumpkin such as *kabocha*, peeled and cut into
   I-inch cubes

2 nearly ripe beefsteak tomatoes

3 cloves garlic, smashed and peeled

salt and pepper to taste

¾ c. water or chicken broth

Heat the lard or oil in a large skillet over a medium-high flame. Add
the chicken and brown quickly on one side, flip over, and add the
onions. Cook until onions just become translucent. Add cumin and stir
well to mix. Place in slow cooker along with the remaining ingredients.
Set slow cooker to low and cook 4 to 6 hours until the meat and
squash are very tender. You may turn the slow cooker to high and
remove cover for the last ½ hour of cooking to slightly thicken the
sauce. Serve hot.

❦ Limas and Lamb Stew

July 1930

Here is a flavorful ode to summer, The Farmer's Wife style. Use young lamb rather than older, tougher mutton for this dish, and sweet new potatoes freshly dug from the ground. You could even use fresh limas, which should be added to the pot about 1 or 2 hours after you've begun cooking,

*to prevent them from going mushy in the pot. For a true Southern flavor,
serve with cornbread or biscuits.*

3 lbs. lamb stew meat, trimmed of fat and cut in cubes
4 slices bacon, cut in pieces
1 large yellow onion, thinly sliced
4 garlic cloves, smashed and peeled
2 large carrots, washed, peeled, and cubed
1 c. water or chicken broth
2 lbs. new potatoes, scrubbed, peeled, and cubed
1 c. dried lima beans, rinsed
salt and pepper to taste
parsley to garnish

Place bacon in a large skillet and fry out over a medium-high flame.
Add the lamb, onions, and carrots. Cook until lamb is browned and
onions are softened. Add garlic just before the onions are done. Place
in slow cooker, deglaze skillet with chicken broth or water, and pour
contents into slow cooker. Add to pot with all remaining ingredients
except parsley. Set slow cooker to low and cook 5 to 6 hours until
meat is very tender. Make sure to keep an eye on the liquid, adding
small additional amounts if necessary. Season to taste. Serve hot with
chopped, fresh parsley for garnish.

Variation: From November 1929 comes this simple variation on the
above, for Ragout of Lamb and Early Vegetables. Substitute 1 pt. small
peeled pickling onions for the yellow onion (you may brown them
quickly on top of the stove before adding to the slow cooker) and
omit the limas. Substitute a few sprinklings of celery salt for some of
the plain salt, add 1 to 2 tbsp. Worcestershire sauce to the pot, and add
the grated rind and juice of 1 lemon just before serving. One-half hour
before the stew is cooked, turn up heat to high and thicken the liquid
with balls made of equal parts butter and flour. Stir in before re-covering
the pot. Season to taste before serving and top with croutons.

❦ Veal Casserole

February 1939

This unthrillingly titled dish is actually a take on two Franco-Russian classics: Beef Stroganoff and Veal Soblianka (a standby at The Russian Tea Room restaurant in New York City). Both dishes make use of meat, mushrooms, and sour cream. No matter which meat you choose to use, you can't go wrong. Since sour cream will break apart from long cooking, mix it into the sauce after cooking for best results.

6 tbsp. butter
1 small yellow onion, chopped
1 lb. mushrooms, stemmed and sliced
2 lbs. veal steak, cubed or sirloin, cut into 1-inch-thick strips
1 tsp. salt
1 tsp. paprika
¼ c. water or chicken broth
1 c. sour cream at room temperature
noodles to serve

In a large skillet, melt butter over a medium heat. Add the onions and cook until just translucent. Add the mushrooms, then the meat, and stir until the meat has lost its pink sheen. Add all to the slow cooker along with the seasonings and water or chicken broth. Set to low and cook 2 to 3 hours until the meat is very tender. Stir in the sour cream and mix well to incorporate. Season to taste and serve hot over buttered noodles.

❧ Delicious Ham Dishes

By Anna Coyle
February 1923

"No other meat food lends itself to quite the variety of dishes as does the ham now hanging in the smokehouse. There are many ways of using ham besides the usual boiled or fried ways. These ways include delicious combinations in casserole dishes, creamed dishes . . . and ham á la King." So said The Farmer's Wife *in February 1923. Indeed, ham was then and continued to be a mainstay of the farm kitchen throughout the tenure of the magazine. The following recipe for "baked" ham is simple and familiar—just the anticipated clove-studding, a bit of brown sugar, and some apple cider to sweeten.*

1 ham, with bone in
15 cloves
¼ c. brown sugar
1 c. apple cider
½ c. raisins (optional)

Rub the ham all over with the brown sugar then stud with cloves. Place in slow cooker and add apple cider. Set slow cooker to low and cook approximately 6 hours until ham is tender. Add raisins if desired and cook an additional ½ hour. Slice to serve.

❧ Pot Roast

May 1933

Tough, inexpensive cuts of meat, like the chuck used in this recipe, are perfect fodder for the slow cooker, which breaks down the sinews of the meat so that a soft, flavorful sort of stew emerges at the end of cooking. The Farmer's Wife never used alcohol of any sort in her cooking, but you may use a bit of red wine instead of vinegar to acidulate the dish. Any sort of root vegetable may be used or excluded here. The Farmer's Wife favored turnips, but carrots and potatoes are the only two vegetables that may be considered a requirement. If you desire, you may thicken the sauce before or after cooking by rolling the meat in flour before browning or after cooking the meat by making balls of equal parts flour and butter and stirring them into the slow cooker on the high setting.

3 to 4 lbs. boneless chuck roast, trimmed of fat
2 tbsp. olive oil
salt and pepper to taste
4 carrots, washed, peeled, and chopped
4 ribs celery, washed and chopped
6 potatoes, washed, peeled, and chopped
1 medium turnip, washed, peeled, and chopped (optional)
2 large yellow onions, peeled and thinly sliced
1½ c. beef broth
¼ c. cider vinegar or red wine
chopped Italian parsley, to garnish

In a large skillet, brown the meat in the olive oil over medium-high flame and sprinkle with salt and pepper, turning the meat as you go. Place in slow cooker with all remaining ingredients except parsley. Set slow cooker to low and cook 7 to 9 hours until meat is very tender. Taste for seasoning and serve hot over buttered noodles. Garnish with chopped parsley, if desired.

For plain meat dishes or when you need to add a little more pep, these sauces are sure to please.

MEAT SAUCES THAT MEN LIKE:
A Plain Dish with a Good Taste Goes Down

By Anna Coyle
January 1923

Men's tastes in matters of food are not quite the same as women's. A study of Friend Husband's favorite meat dishes should include relishes, sauces, and spicy flavors which, added to the ordinary meat dish, transform it into something not ordinary at all.

Sauces that give variety to meat dishes are especially welcome at this season when there is likely to be an abundance of beef or pork on hand after killing.

With beef serve these sauces: parsley, mushroom, horseradish, tomato, Creole, chili, Worcestershire, chow chow, or Maître D'Hotel butter.

With lamb serve: mint sauce, caper sauce, currant jelly, or mint jelly.

With pork serve: tart apple sauce, apple jelly, or apricot sauce.

Serve cranberry sauce with turkey, currant jelly with roast chicken, and apple sauce with roast duck.

CREOLE SAUCE

2 tbsp. onion, chopped
4 tbsp. green pepper, finely chopped
2 tbsp. butter
2 tbsp. flour
1 c. crushed tomato
1 c. brown meat stock
salt and pepper

Cook onion and pepper with the butter 5 minutes, stir in flour, and gradually add tomatoes and meat stock. Cook 15 minutes.

HORSERADISH SAUCE

4 tbsp. grated horseradish
½ tsp. salt
⅛ tsp. pepper
½ tsp. dried mustard
1 tsp. sugar
1 tbsp. vinegar
1 c. whipped cream

Combine first 6 ingredients and fold into the whipped cream.

❧ Pork Roast
September 1926

*This recipe for roast pork and the one for beef pot roast that precedes
it are plain, everyday fare that the farmer's wife cooked up for ordinary
winter dinners. Almost any sort of herb or seasoning can be added to
change the nature of the dish. Feel free to experiment with other flavors
when straightforward ones will not do. Or, enliven the plain roasts with one
of the sauces listed in the sidebar on the previous and following pages.
Sauces, such as the ones the magazine published in January 1923, as well
as homemade pickles and other
condiments, were the farmer's
wife's main trick in adding zip to
otherwise modest meals.*

3 lbs. pork loin roast, trimmed
   of fat
1 small yellow onion, peeled
   and thinly sliced
1 tbsp. olive oil
1 c. chicken or vegetable stock
bay leaf
salt and pepper to taste

Brown roast in olive oil with
the onion. Place roast and
onion in slow cooker, then
deglaze pan with stock. Add
salt and pepper to taste and
bay leaf. Set slow cooker to
low and cook 5 to 7 hours
until the meat is very tender.

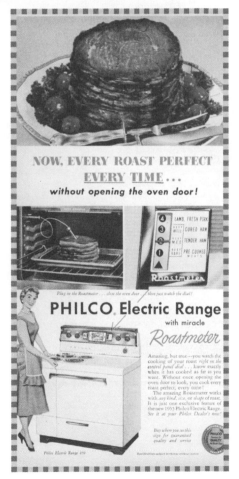

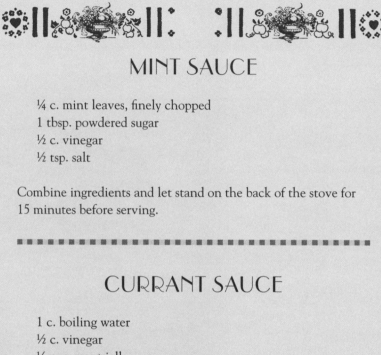

MINT SAUCE

¼ c. mint leaves, finely chopped
1 tbsp. powdered sugar
½ c. vinegar
½ tsp. salt

Combine ingredients and let stand on the back of the stove for 15 minutes before serving.

CURRANT SAUCE

1 c. boiling water
½ c. vinegar
½ c. currant jelly
1 c. currants, chopped
1 tbsp. flour

Heat water, vinegar, currant jelly, and currant together and simmer for 10 minutes. Thicken with flour rubbed to a smooth paste in a little cold water. Cook thoroughly.

CAPER SAUCE

½ c. butter
1½ c. hot water or mutton broth
2 tbsp. flour
½ tsp. salt
½ c. capers, drained

Melt half the butter, stir in the flour, and gradually add the hot liquid, stirring constantly. Add the salt and the remaining butter and capers just before serving.

MAÎTRE D'HOTEL BUTTER

¼ c. butter
½ tsp. salt
⅛ tsp. pepper
½ tbsp. parsley, finely chopped
¾ tbsp. lemon juice

Cream the butter and mix in salt, pepper, and parsley, then lemon juice very slowly.

Side Dishes

❦ Boston Baked Beans

May 1930

Here is a Farmer's Wife *standby, variations of which appear in the magazine more than once a year.* The Farmer's Wife *usually added molasses only to her beans, although the result may not be quite sweet enough for some palates. You can add an equal amount of brown sugar or maple syrup if you have more of a sweet tooth. Dried mustard is more typical of* The Farmer's Wife, *but prepared mustard helps thicken the sauce and lends a much-needed tinge of acidity.*

1 qt. small white beans
1 onion, chopped
4 strips bacon or 4-inch-strip salt pork, sliced thin
½ c. molasses
½ c. brown sugar or maple syrup
5 cloves
2 tbsp. Dijon mustard
2 c. boiling water
2 tsp. salt

Soak the beans overnight in enough cold water to cover. Drain and add to slow cooker. Fry the onion with the bacon or salt pork in a skillet over high heat until the fat is rendered from the meat and the onion is translucent. Drain and add to slow cooker along with remaining ingredients, except for salt. Set slow cooker to low and cook 8 hours until beans are tender. If desired, set slow cooker to high and remove lid for 30 additional minutes to thicken liquid. Add salt and serve.

Turkish Pilaf
March 1934

Rice is oh-so-easy to cook in the slow cooker, especially if you do not possess a rice cooker. It doesn't take long: only about half an hour, which is the same time you would spend cooking rice on top of the stove. But perfect rice is easier to accomplish in the slow cooker, especially if you resist the urge to open the cover and stir the rice around. Again, a burner on the stove is freed up for cooking other tasty things for the dinner table. The Farmer's Wife, both in this version and another that ran in the magazine in May 1927, added ground beef to her pilaf. This is a vegetarian version, unless you choose to add chicken stock.

1 small yellow onion, thinly sliced
1 tbsp. olive oil
2 c. long-grain rice, such as basmati, rinsed
2 c. tomatoes, finely chopped
4 c. water or stock
1 tsp. salt
2 tbsp. butter
Parmesan cheese, to serve
parsley or cilantro, to garnish

In a large skillet, heat the olive oil over medium flame and cook the onion until it is translucent. Add the rice and stir to mix. Add to the slow cooker along with the remaining ingredients except the cheese and garnish. Set slow cooker to low and cook about 30 minutes until all the liquid is absorbed. Allow the rice to sit covered for an additional 15 to 30 minutes. Serve hot out of the pot, topped with grated Parmesan cheese, if you desire, and chopped Italian parsley, or chopped cilantro.

❧ Candied Orange Sweet Potatoes

April 1931

The important thing in this recipe is not how thick the sweet potatoes are sliced (although the thicker they are the longer they take to cook), but that the slices are of a uniform thickness for even cooking. The vegetable mandolin is a perfect tool for this. These sweet potatoes can be enjoyed in the cool of autumn when sweet potatoes are just ripening or even in late summer. The slow cooker means no hot oven to contend with. The Farmer's Wife favored casseroles of this sort, and here two recipes have been spliced together. One is simple and seasoned with salt, pepper, and butter. The other incorporates orange for a slightly zestier flavor. You can also add firm, tart apples that are peeled and sliced in equal proportion to sweet potatoes. Add the apples and sweet potatoes to the slow cooker in alternating layers.

2 large sweet potatoes, peeled and sliced ¼-inch thick
1 tsp. salt
¼ c. melted unsalted butter, plus extra for buttering the inside of the
  slow cooker
¼ c. brown sugar
½ tsp. grated orange zest

Butter the inside of the slow cooker and arrange sweet potatoes
inside it in layers, overlapping slightly. Sprinkle with salt, pour butter
over evenly, then sprinkle with sugar and orange zest. Set slow
cooker to low and cook 4 hours. Serve immediately.

SCALLOPED TOMATOES

April 1910

Put a layer of canned tomato in a well-buttered baking dish. Season with salt and pepper, sprinkle over it 1 tsp. sugar, then add a layer of breadcrumbs, another of tomato, seasoning as before, and so on until the tomato is all used. Put dots of butter over the top layer of bread.

If you happen to have a quantity of dried bread on hand (every scrap of bread should be saved and dried for such purposes), it may always be used for scalloping vegetables by soaking it first in cold water until soft; then squeeze out and use as directed above.

❧ Scalloped Tomatoes
April 1910

There is very little variation necessary to adapt the sidebar recipe for scalloped tomatoes for the slow cooker. A little minced garlic is added for pungency, and Parmesan cheese is added to the breadcrumbs to aid in the flavoring. Breadcrumbs are sprinkled on the top layer of the dish only, as they have a tendency to become gluey in between layers. This is a great summer treat. Be sure to serve hot.

1 tbsp. plus 1 tsp. butter
3 to 4 large beefsteak tomatoes (enough to make 3 layers), ripe but
   still firm
¾ tsp. salt
⅓ tsp. sugar
1 tsp. minced fresh garlic
freshly ground black pepper
⅓ c. breadcrumbs
2 tbsp. grated Parmesan cheese

Butter the inside of the slow cooker with 1 tsp. of butter. Core the tomatoes, cut them in half, and slice in ¼-inch slices. Place them in one slightly overlapping layer at the bottom of the slow cooker and sprinkle with ⅓ of the salt and sugar, half the garlic, and a little black pepper. Repeat with a second layer, then a third. Mix the breadcrumbs with the cheese and sprinkle over the top of the tomatoes. Dot with the remaining butter and set to cook on low for 2½ hours and uncover for the last ½ hour of cooking. Serve immediately.

❧ Escalloped Eggplant with Tomatoes and Onions
August 1927

This is an easy, hearty, late-summer dish that can be cooked up in the slow cooker without adding heat to your already hot house or apartment. Use ripe but firm beefsteak tomatoes and large eggplants, which contain fewer seeds than the small ones.

2 large yellow onions, thinly sliced
2 tbsp. olive oil
2 large purple eggplants, peeled and cut into ½-inch slices
4 to 6 large, ripe but firm beefsteak tomatoes, sliced
salt and pepper
unsalted butter

Heat the olive oil in a large skillet and cook the onions till they are translucent and just beginning to turn golden. Butter the inside of the slow cooker. Place a layer of eggplant on the bottom and top with a layer of tomatoes then a coating of onions, sprinkle with salt and pepper, and dot with butter at each layer. Continue until all the vegetables are used. Sprinkle on a final bit of salt and pepper, and a dotting of butter. Set slow cooker to low and cook 2 to 3 hours until the vegetables are tender but still hold their shape. If they begin to stick to the bottom of the dish during cooking, you may add 1 tbsp. of water.

❦ Cauliflower in Tomato Sauce

October 1918

Here's a simple cauliflower dish, which can be made slightly fancier with the addition of herbs—fresh thyme, rosemary, or sage. Be sure to serve with chopped parsley and a lot of buttered bread.

1 large head cauliflower, broken into florets
1 small onion, peeled and thinly sliced
2 tbsp. olive oil
1 c. crushed tomatoes
salt and pepper to taste
fresh herbs, if desired, plus fresh chopped parsley to garnish

Cut cauliflower into florets and parboil in salted water for 2 minutes (this will help preserve some of the vegetable's vitamin content, but is not absolutely necessary if you are strapped for time). Drain and put in slow cooker. Meanwhile, cook onion in olive oil until lightly browned. Add to slow cooker with remaining ingredients except parsley. Set slow cooker to low and cook 2 to 3 hours until cauliflower is nicely tender. Check for seasonings and serve. Garnish with parsley.

SAUSAGE SUPPER DISH

Photo. Farm Journal

❦ Succotash
February 1922

Alan Davidson points out that this classic old American dish, thought by most to be a vegetarian offering, included two chickens, plus corned beef and pork in its first recorded recipe; bear meat was included in a slightly later recipe. Although recipes with salt pork or bacon still turn up from time to time, it is still generally accepted that succotash, no matter what else is added to it, is a dish consisting of lima beans and corn. In fact, its name is taken from a Narragansett word (msickquatash, according to Merriam-Webster) meaning "boiled corn kernels". Fresh lima beans and corn would be ideal ingredients for this dish, but frozen limas and corn or dried limas may be substituted, although expect a longer cooking time for the latter. Succotash was a great favorite of The Farmer's Wife—this is one of only ten or twelve varieties she published over the years.

1 pt. shelled fresh lima beans
1 pt. corn, cut from the cob (about 4 ears)
4 tbsp. unsalted butter
1 tbsp. water
1 tsp. sugar
salt and pepper to taste
¼ c. half-and-half

Place all ingredients except half-and-half in slow cooker. Set slow cooker to low and cook 2 to 2½ hours until vegetables are almost tender. Season to taste, add half-and-half, and stir to mix. Cook an additional ½ hour. Serve hot.

❧ Cabbage and Chestnuts

❧ Cabbage with Celery Seeds

❧ Cabbage with Bacon
January 1929

"Cabbages and kings"—of course, and why not? There are so many delicious ways to prepare the lowly cabbage that it may be lifted far above the humble plane that it occupies in the mind of many. Special consideration is due to cabbage for its gift of vitamins.

"The French use chestnuts with cabbage to make a very appetizing dish. The chestnut, which is high in starch content, is more widely used as a vegetable in Europe than it is in this country, but American housewives are becoming familiar with this article of food." So said The Farmer's Wife *in January 1929 in an extensive article on the use of cabbage. Below is a recipe that can be mixed and matched from three recipes that ran with that article and used chestnuts, celery seeds, and/or bacon to vary the dish. A fabulous modern concession that was not available to* The Farmer's Wife *is jarred chestnuts, already roasted and peeled, which eliminates all the work of roasting them yourself and sacrifices none of the flavor.*

4 slices bacon, chopped and fried out (optional)
1 small head red cabbage, shredded (about 8 c.)
1 15-oz. jar roasted chestnuts (about 2½ c.), broken into pieces
1 tsp. salt
pepper to taste
1 c. apple juice

1 tsp. celery seed heated in 1 tbsp. olive oil, for serving (optional)
Put the bacon (if using), cabbage, chestnuts, salt, pepper, and apple juice into the slow cooker. Stir to mix. Set slow cooker to low and cook 4 hours until the cabbage is very tender. Adjust seasoning. If desired, toss with celery seeds in olive oil just before serving. Best eaten hot, but it can also be reheated the next day for leftovers.

HARVEST TIME SHORTCUTS

July 1936

Tradition has a way of asserting itself at harvest time. In the
harvest meal contest conducted last year by *The Farmer's Wife
Magazine*, we found that the meals planned by farm homemakers
in 35 states fell into pretty general patterns. As we summarized it,
"Hungry men do not care for fancy dishes. They want plenty of
good food, well cooked." So we compiled menus and recipes
in a booklet called "Feeding Hungry Folks" and therein are
general favorites in attractive menus, accompanied by large
quantity recipes.

When the harvesters were a long distance from the house,
the noon meal was sometimes taken to the field. A Utah
contributor wrote that their ranch was six miles from their home,
so a hearty breakfast and evening dinner were served at their
house, with a lighter noon meal sent with the men when they
left in the morning.

❦ Spoon Corn Bread
November 1911

This is a classic American dish with roots in many directions: south to the Aztecs and east to England. Traditionally, it is soft and light thanks to the addition of baking powder. Fine-ground cornmeal also helps keep it on the delicate side. As a rule it also generally eschews the use of sugar, although contemporary corn bread lovers who have grown accustomed to more sweetish stuff may wish to add a bit of sweetener.

2 c. milk
½ c. fine-ground cornmeal
2 eggs
1 tbsp. melted butter or oil, plus extra for greasing the slow cooker
1 tsp. baking powder
½ tsp. salt
1 to 2 tbsp. sugar, if desired

Butter the inside of the slow cooker. Add all ingredients to the slow cooker and whisk very well to incorporate. Make sure that the eggs and baking powder especially are beaten in. Set slow cooker to low and cook about 3 hours until just set. To serve, spoon onto plates right from the pot, nice and hot.

❦ Corn Pudding

November 1912

2 heaping c. corn kernels, fresh or frozen
3 eggs
2 tbsp. sugar
1 tbsp. butter, plus extra for greasing the slow cooker
1½ c. milk
large pinch salt

Heavily butter the inside of the slow cooker. Add 1½ c. of corn into slow cooker; finely chop remaining ½ c. corn and add. Mix remaining ingredients in a large bowl. Add to corn. Set slow cooker to low and cook 2 hours until just set. Serve hot.

BAKED STUFFED ZUCCHINI

Eva's Mexican Beef Hash from freezer is ready in oven when she gets home from town (round trip takes an hour).

TUNA BAKE

RANCH-STYLE CHICKEN

❦ Green Pea Pudding
July 1912

This sweet and delicious side dish, a variation on the above Corn Pudding recipe, is sure to be a family favorite. The Farmer's Wife would have used fresh shell peas from her garden, but frozen small sweet peas are more consistently sweet, less starchy, and are recommended here.

2 tbsp. unsalted butter, melted, plus extra (unmelted) for buttering the
   inside of the slow cooker
3 c. frozen peas
3 eggs
2 c. half-and-half
salt and pepper to taste

Butter the inside of the slow cooker. Purée 1 c. of peas with the half-and-half in the blender and mix in remaining ingredients. Pour into slow cooker and set to low. Cook 2 hours until just set.
Serve immediately.

❄ Normandy Carrots

November 1931

This sweet-and-sour dish, once popular with lunching ladies, has fallen out of favor in recent years. There is scant reference to it in cookbooks or food histories, which leaves some speculation as to its origins. This writer's best guess: Normandy, a region in northern France famous for apples and butter, once inspired numbers of recipes using both products. This recipe incorporated butter, of course, and vinegar—no doubt originally apple cider vinegar—the sharpness of which was cut by the addition of sugar. It is a nice complement to a roast or pork chops.

1 lb. (approximately 4 c.) carrots, washed, peeled, and cut thinly in
　2-inch strips
¼ c. sugar
¼ c. vinegar
2 tbsp. butter
¼ tsp. salt

Add all ingredients to the slow cooker. Mix well. Set slow cooker to low and cook 3 to 4 hours (depending on the age and thickness of the carrots), until carrots are tender all the way through.

❧ Spiced Cranberries

December 1931

During the holidays when stove space is at a premium, the slow cooker is perfect for dishes such as this one, especially when the whole meal must be put together at the same time.

4 c. cranberries
1½ c. brown sugar
½ c. mild vinegar
¼ c. water
1 tsp. paprika
1 tsp. cinnamon
½ tsp. ground cloves
½ tsp. salt

Add all ingredients to the slow cooker. Set to low and cook 2 hours. Raise the temperature to high, remove cover, and cook an additional ½ to 1 hour to reduce cooking liquid. Serve hot or cold.

Variation: Stewed Cranberries, a bare-bones holiday dish from November 1910: Stew 4 c. cranberries with 2 c. sugar and ½ c. water in slow cooker on low for 2 to 2½ hours. Remove cover and cook on high for ½ to 1 hour, if necessary, to reduce cooking liquid.

Puts an end to last-minute oven juggling

The roast won't have to wait for the cake

(NOR THE BISCUITS OR PIES FOR THE ROAST)

Bar-B-Kewer (SEPARATE MEAT OVEN) *will broil roasts*

(ALSO WHOLE HAMS, CHICKENS, TURKEYS)

Leaving oven free for baking... at the same time

ESTATE *Heatrola* RANGES
GAS & ELECTRIC

Desserts

Lipped preserving kettle, 9 to 20 quarts. 65c to $2.25. Tin lining or...

❦ Coconut Bread Pudding

September 1923

This is a wonderful way to use up leftover bread, which is something nearly every household seems to accumulate in one form or another. It certainly did in the household of The Farmer's Wife. Recipes for bread pudding appear in the magazine with amazing frequency. Some are plain, some incorporate fruits and nuts or various extracts; this slightly tropical one has coconut. Heels from sliced loaves, half a baguette left a day too long in the bag, and even bits of pumpernickel bagel can be stored in a resealable bag in the freezer until enough has accumulated to translate into this classic American dessert. Thaw thoroughly before attempting to cube the bread!

unsalted butter
4 c. stale bread cubes
1 c. shredded unsweetened
   coconut
2 eggs
1½ c. milk
½ c. heavy cream
1 c. sugar
1 tbsp. vanilla extract

THIS NATIVE GIRL

Butter the inside of the slow cooker, add bread and coconut, and mix together. In a bowl, whisk up the remaining ingredients and pour over bread and coconut. (Note: the custard should thoroughly soak the bread. If it does not, add extra cream and milk until all the bread cubes can be moistened.) Set the slow cooker on low and cook for 2½ hours. Remove the lid for the last ½ hour to enhance the crust. Best served warm right out of the slow cooker with a little heavy cream poured over or a small scoop of ice cream.

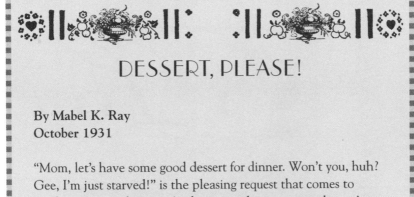

DESSERT, PLEASE!

By Mabel K. Ray
October 1931

"Mom, let's have some good dessert for dinner. Won't you, huh? Gee, I'm just starved!" is the pleasing request that comes to mothers time and again. And to meet those requests, haven't you leafed through your cookbooks to find something a little different but without seeing any? There are so many interesting but simple recipes in the bulletins that come to my desk that I'll be your second eyesight—with your permission—and select some recipes we'll all enjoy.

Here are a few more varieties of Bread Pudding that ran in the magazine over the years.

■■■

❦ Plain Bread Pudding
May 1913

unsalted butter
4 c. stale bread cubes
2 eggs
1½ c. milk
½ c. heavy cream
1 c. sugar
1 tbsp. lemon extract

Follow the directions for Coconut Bread Pudding. Serve with 3 bananas mashed and whipped until frothy.

■■■

❦ Caramel Bread Pudding

December 1911

unsalted butter
4 c. stale bread cubes
2 eggs
1½ c. milk
½ c. heavy cream
1 c. brown sugar
1 tbsp. cinnamon

Follow directions for Coconut Bread
Pudding. Serve hot.

❦ Raisin and Chocolate Bread Pudding
March 1924

unsalted butter
4 c. stale bread cubes
2 eggs
1½ c. milk
½ c. heavy cream
¾ c. sugar
1 square bittersweet Baker's chocolate, grated
1 c. raisins
1 tbsp. vanilla
grating of nutmeg

Follow directions for Coconut Bread Pudding, mixing all ingredients together except nutmeg, which should be grated over the top ½ hour before the dish is finished. Serve hot.

APPLES STAGE A COMEBACK

By Meta Given
October 1938

Turning the pages of immortal literature down the centuries, we find mention of many fruits of tree and vine—olives, pomegranates, grapes, melons, "apricocks," and peaches—but the fruit which has evoked the most eloquence from the literary great of our own land is the modest apple.

One of the major tragedies of the twentieth century is that modern children go for snacks to five-cent candy bars instead of juicy apples, and that mother no longer remembers what her mother did to make apples pies a fit subject for poets, essayists, and even eminent divines. Yet the apples are just the same today; a steady stream of them from June to March of every year, red-cheeked or enameled in green or gold or stripes; white fleshed or pale green or yellow or gold; crisp and juicy and tart or sweet and mealy—apples for every taste and every purpose.

New ways of cooking apples are not what is needed. Stewed apples and applesauce and apple betty that have delighted generations of Americans still delight this generation, when they can get them.

❦ Prune Bread Pudding

October 1931

unsalted butter
4 c. stale bread cubes
2 c. cooked dried prunes
2 eggs
¾ c. sugar
1½ c. milk
½ c. heavy cream
½ c. prune juice
1 tsp. cinnamon
1 tbsp. grated orange peel

Follow directions for Coconut Bread Pudding. Serve hot.

❦ Brown Betty

May 1929

The Farmer's Wife *did not let much go to waste in her kitchen. She used and reused as much as she could, turning leftover once-fresh bread into breadcrumbs, which turn up again and again in her chops and casseroles and desserts. She and her family gobbled up fresh*

*fruit in season from her garden and orchard, but she also never failed to
cook up the less gorgeous produce (windfall apples, for example) with its
knobs and bumps and bruises. This is not to say that her aim was thrift
alone. As this recipe attests, a decidedly delicious dessert can be made
from the dregs, along with a few staples from the larder.*

1 c. breadcrumbs
2 tbsp. melted butter, plus more (unmelted) for buttering
  the slow cooker
1 c. sugar
grated zest of 1 lemon
1 tsp. cinnamon
5 sour windfall apples, such as Granny Smith
juice of 1 lemon
heavy cream

Butter the inside of the slow cooker. In a bowl, mix the breadcrumbs
with the melted butter, ½ c. of the sugar, zest, and cinnamon. Peel and
chop the apples into ½-inch cubes, place in a bowl, and mix with the
lemon juice and remaining sugar. Spread half the breadcrumb mixture
on the bottom of the slow cooker. Top with the apples and then the
remaining breadcrumbs. Set the slow cooker to low and cook covered
for 2 hours, then cook uncovered for an additional ½ hour. Serve hot
with a drizzling of heavy cream.

Variation: Prune Betty from February 1932: Substitute 1½ c. cooked
and pitted prunes, roughly chopped, for the apples.

❧ Stewed Rhubarb

April 1925

The slow cooker is a real advantage when you have a large crop of rhubarb coming in from the garden in early spring. Stew it (see below) to eat over whipped cream as a simple dessert, use it straight from the pot, or store in the refrigerator or freezer for later use as a pie filling.

4 c. rhubarb, diced fine
1 c. sugar
1 tbsp. lemon juice
¼ c. water

Place all ingredients in the slow cooker. Set to low and cook 3 to 4 hours until tender. Check the water from time to time to make sure the bottom of the slow cooker is damp and that the rhubarb is not sticking to the pot. To serve, allow it to cool and spoon onto beds of freshly whipped, lightly sweetened cream.

Variation: From April 1926 comes this variation: Add ¼ to ½ c. seedless raisins to the above recipe.

❦ Indian Pudding

February 1910

This dessert is a classic American dish that originated with colonial cooks in the mid-1700s. Not surprisingly, it appears on the pages of The Farmer's Wife *with great frequency, as it was already considered a "classic" dish, even at the turn of the nineteenth century. Some food historians claim it is a variation of the English hasty pudding, with cornmeal ("Indian meal," hence the name Indian pudding) replacing wheat or oats here in the New World. Those who could afford sugar used it to sweeten this dish, but less-expensive molasses was more common. These days it is usually baked, although originally it was often boiled in cloth bags, as ovens were scarce. It benefits from slow cooking, which makes it a perfect candidate for the slow cooker.*

⅔ c. cornmeal
1 qt. milk
½ tsp. salt
1 tsp. powdered ginger
2 eggs
pinch baking soda
½ c. molasses
1 tbsp. butter, plus extra for greasing the slow cooker
1 c. mixed dried chopped raisins, currants, dates, and figs

Butter the slow cooker, add all the ingredients, and whisk. Make sure the eggs are well beaten. Set the slow cooker on low and cook 2 to 3 hours until set. Overcooking will result in a wet, curdled mess. This pudding may not be sweet enough for some, in which case you may serve with vanilla ice cream or a sprinkling of brown sugar.

❦ Lemon Rice Pudding

February 1910

A true comfort food dessert, rice pudding has origins dating back to the ancient Romans, according to food historian Alan Davidson. Originally prepared as a food for invalids, rice pudding today still has a soothing quality about it. This lemony version was cooked up in the February 1910 issue. Basmati rice is used here for a delicate texture. For a pudding in which the grains are distinct, you may shorten the cooking time. For a more porridgelike consistency, lengthen the cooking time. Whichever type of pudding you prefer, be sure to serve it hot.

unsalted butter
¾ c. basmati rice, rinsed and drained
½ c. sugar
1 egg
grated zest of 1 lemon
3 c. milk

Butter the inside of the slow cooker, then add all the ingredients. Whisk well, making sure the egg is well beaten-in. Set slow cooker to low and cook 2 to 3 hours, till desired consistency. Serve hot.

Variations: Rice Pudding is a farmer's wife's favorite dessert, bypassing even Bread Pudding in popularity. The following pages offer several types of Rice Pudding.

❦ Rice and Apricot Pudding

February 1910

This recipe uses the same process as Lemon Rice Pudding.

unsalted butter
¾ c. basmati rice, rinsed and drained
½ c. sugar
1 egg
grated zest of 1 lemon
3 c. milk

Omit lemon rind. Mix remaining ingredients with 2 crumbled
macaroons and ½ c. finely chopped dried apricots. Serve hot
with apricot sauce: Mix 1 c. apricot juice with ½ c. sugar and 1 tsp.
cornstarch. Boil 5 minutes and strain.

Praises Dry Yeast's Spee...

Farmwife is Prize-winning Cook

Fifty-two prizes in 3 years— that's the impressive record set by prize-cook Mrs. Joseph J. Rizzo. This Cedar Falls, Iowa farmwife is the busy mother of three children, including twins Peter and Paula (above). Yet she finds time to enter and win both State and County Fair Contests. Her latest triumph came at the 1950 State Fair where she won eight prizes in three different classifications.

Like so many top cooks, Mrs. Rizzo has *one* favorite yeast— Fleischmann's Active Dry Yeast. "It's so fast—and easy to use," she says. "I depend on this grand dry yeast for prize-winning results."

Everybody loves it—that deliciously *different* flavor of yeast-raised treats. So good to eat—so good for you, too. When you bake at home—do it with yeast—the very best yeast. Fleischmann's Active Dry Yeast is so fast rising, so easy to use—and always dependable! Buy a supply. You'll like it!

❧ Fig Rice Pudding
December 1911

This recipe uses the same process as Lemon Rice Pudding.

unsalted butter
¾ c. basmati rice, rinsed and drained
½ c. sugar
1 egg
grated zest of 1 lemon
3 c. milk

Add ½ c. chopped dried figs. Substitute ¼ c. light brown sugar and ¼ c. maple syrup for white sugar. Instead of mixing in with grated lemon zest, use it as a serving garnish. Serve hot.

ARE YOU A CLOCK CHASER?

❦ Pennsylvania Rice Pudding

August 1921

This recipe uses the same process as Lemon Rice Pudding.

unsalted butter
¾ c. basmati rice, rinsed and drained
½ c. sugar
1 egg
grated zest of 1 lemon
3 c. milk

Omit lemon zest. Add ⅓ c. raisins and ½ tsp. nutmeg.

❧ Rice Pudding with Dates

May 1927

This recipe uses the same process as Lemon Rice Pudding.

unsalted butter
¾ c. basmati rice, rinsed and drained
½ c. sugar
1 egg
grated zest of 1 lemon
3 c. milk

Omit lemon zest. Substitute brown sugar for white and add ⅓ c. finely chopped dates.

❦ Banana Pudding

May 1913

This is comfort food at its most comforting. Warm, sweet banana pudding will surely appeal to every member of your family on hot or cool nights. An important factor is texture; the banana must be mashed smooth (or puréed in the blender with a little of the milk you will use for cooking) or the ensuing lumps will detract from the satisfaction of the pudding. This recipe makes enough to feed a crowd. The Farmer's Wife would have used the leftover egg whites for a meringue topping, but this tends to get soggy in the slow cooker. You can make meringue cookies in the conventional oven or serve the pudding with 'Nilla Wafers.

⅔ c. grated breadcrumbs
2 c. well-mashed banana (about 6 small or 4 medium bananas)
finely grated rind of 2 lemons
4 egg yolks
2 c. milk
1 c. sugar

Butter the inside of the slow cooker. Add all ingredients and mix well to incorporate. Set slow cooker to low and cook 2 to 3 hours until set. Serve hot.

❦ Graham Pudding

September 1926

This so-called "pudding" is more of a cake and may be accomplished in much the same way as the English Gingerbread Cake that follows it. Graham flour is a type of coarsely ground whole wheat flour that is readily available in health and specialty stores (not to be confused with gram flour, which refers to a flour made from ground chickpeas).

¼ c. butter, plus extra for buttering the inside of the slow cooker
½ c. molasses
1 c. graham flour
½ c. cornmeal
3 tsp. baking powder
½ tsp. baking soda
1 tsp. salt
1 tsp. cinnamon
½ tsp. each mace, cloves, allspice, ginger
½ c. buttermilk
⅔ c. raisins

Cream butter, add molasses, and stir. Mix and sift dry ingredients; add alternately with buttermilk to butter mixture. Stir in raisins. Heavily butter the inside of the slow cooker. Pour in batter and set slow cooker to low. Cook 2 to 3 hours until the pudding is set. Serve hot with whipped cream, if desired.

❧ English Gingerbread Cake
March 1916

Baked goods are a wonderful category of foods to make in the slow cooker. I tested this recipe on a blisteringly hot July day, without ever turning on my oven. The result? A lovely cake in a still-cool summer apartment. The Farmer's Wife was a huge proponent of gingerbread. She had dozens and dozens of recipes for it—in cake and cookie form, hard and soft, frosted and not. This recipe includes raisins and nuts for a rich, chewy variety.

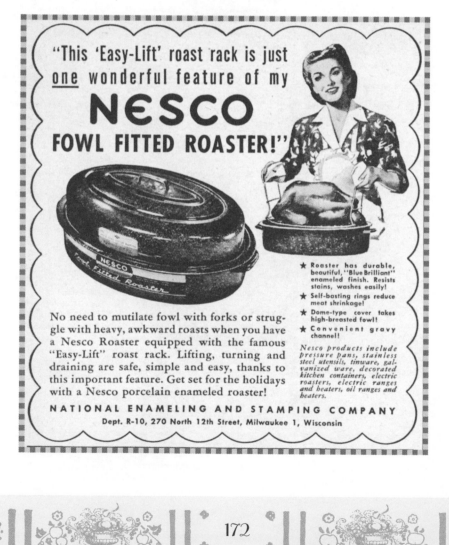

Take note: The gingerbread in the oblong slow cooker tends to cook first at the edges and last in the center. So, be sure to keep a close eye on the cake, turning it off and removing it from the slow cooker just as soon as the center is set, otherwise you will end up with very dry edges. Also helpful is wrapping a thin dishtowel around the underside of the cover and tucking it up over the top edges, to catch any condensation that develops during cooking.

1¾ c. flour
½ c. raisins
½ c. chopped walnuts
½ tsp. baking soda
½ c. unsalted butter, plus more for buttering the inside of the slow
   cooker
1 c. molasses
½ c. sugar
2 eggs
1½ tsp. cinnamon
1½ tsp. cloves
1 tsp. ground ginger

Heavily butter the inside of the slow cooker. Mix all ingredients together in a large bowl and pour into the slow cooker. Set to low and cook 2½ to 3 hours, stirring a bit before the mixture sets. Keeping a close eye on the cake, remove it just as soon as the center is set. Immediately remove with a spatula and place on a rack to cool.

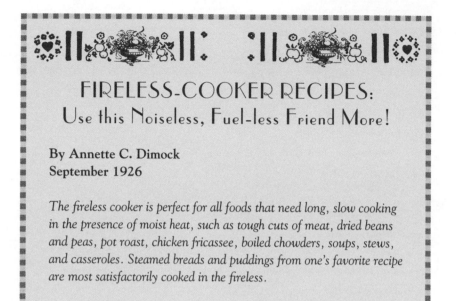

FIRELESS-COOKER RECIPES:
Use this Noiseless, Fuel-less Friend More!

By Annette C. Dimock
September 1926

The fireless cooker is perfect for all foods that need long, slow cooking in the presence of moist heat, such as tough cuts of meat, dried beans and peas, pot roast, chicken fricassee, boiled chowders, soups, stews, and casseroles. Steamed breads and puddings from one's favorite recipe are most satisfactorily cooked in the fireless.

❧ Cranberry Pudding
January 1911

This is a pudding in the English tradition—as Dr. Johnson defined it, containing flour, milk, and eggs—rather than the now-strictly American interpretation (i.e., rice pudding, tapioca pudding, chocolate pudding) that the English would define as a "milk pudding." It is technically steamed in the slow cooker and is quite delicate and sweet. Contemporary cooks may be inclined to make this during the holiday season, due to the presence of cranberries. However, it is worth noting that The Farmer's Wife made this in January 1911, and another variation (see below) appeared in September 1926. This writer tested both recipes in late sweltering July, which was possible thanks to the modern convenience of frozen foods. It made a very welcome conclusion to a light summer meal, especially since any such confection baked in the oven would have been out of the question during that season.

7 tbsp. unsalted butter, plus extra for greasing the slow cooker
2 eggs
¾ c. plus 1 tbsp. milk
1 8-oz. package (approximately 2 c.) cranberries, fresh or frozen
1½ c. sugar
3 c. flour
2 tsp. baking powder

Cream together the butter, milk, and sugar in a blender. Pour the mixture over the cranberries, add the sugar, and sift in the flour and baking powder. Mix very well and turn out into the well-buttered slow cooker. Set to low and cook 3 to 4 hours until just set in the center. Serve with heavy cream and dust with nutmeg.

Variation: In this version of Cranberry Pudding from September 1926, substitute buttermilk for whole milk, and ½ tsp. baking soda for an equal amount of the baking powder to neutralize the acid in the buttermilk.

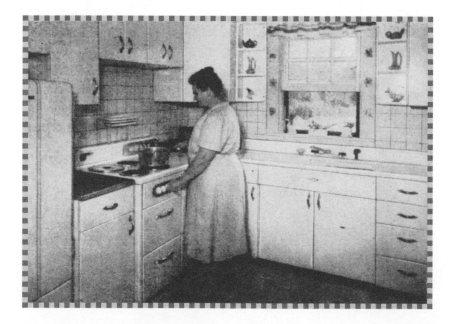

❦ Poached Pears

January 1926

This is a rather gentrified departure for The Farmer's Wife *in the realm of desserts. It can be served any time pears are in season, for any occasion whatsoever. You can even skip the whipped cream for a more refreshing effect.*

4 ripe but firm pears, such as Bosc, peeled, cored, and halved
2 c. water
1 c. sugar
1 tbsp. lemon rind, grated

In a pot on top of the stove, make a syrup of the water, sugar, and lemon rind by boiling all together until it just begins to thicken. Add to slow cooker along with pears and set to low. Cook 2 to 3 hours until the pears are just tender, stirring occasionally to ensure that the fruit sits in the syrup on all sides. Serve hot with the syrup and sweetened, freshly whipped cream.

Variation: From November 1931, Crème de Menthe Pears: Substitute ½ tsp. mint oil for the lemon rind.

❦ Caramel Raisin Apple

February 1922

Baked apples are a classic winter treat, and they are so easily made in the slow cooker. They will take quite a bit longer to slow-cook than to bake, but as always with the slow cooker, this means you will have oven space readily available for another baking task.

6 large, firm, tart apples, well washed
½ c. raisins
1 c. light brown sugar
2 tbsp. unsalted butter, plus extra for buttering the slow cooker
½ c. apple juice

Core the apples and peel a bit of the skin from the top. Mix the raisins and sugar together and pack the mixture into the apples. Top each apple with a pat of butter. Butter the slow cooker and arrange the apples inside. Add the apple juice to cover the bottom of the pot. Set the slow cooker to low and cook 4 to 6 hours until the apples are softened through. According to *The Farmer's Wife*, these "may be served hot or cold, with or without cream."

Meat is higher— Fish is Plentiful

HERE ARE TASTY NEW WAYS TO SERVE THEM BOTH

"Livestock prices in 1935 . . . expected to be highest since 1930."
Dept. of Agriculture, Misc. Pub. No. 215

"Fish now being sold in a great many stores where it has never been before."
Atlantic Coast Fisheries

FISH is now plentiful. Housewives are greeting it with delight as meat gets more expensive. They are cleverly varying their menus with fish and the less expensive meat cuts. The budget is balanced and meals were never better.

This new resourcefulness in cooking has led housewives to Pyrex Ovenware. In these good-looking dishes, food can be cooked in delicious gravies.

Saves Effort . . . Fuel . . . Time

It actually cuts down kitchen hours, too. Food cooks an average of 20% sooner and down go fuel costs. One sparkling dish can be used for cooking—serving—then goes into the refrigerator.

Pyrex Brand Ovenware is priced at its lowest now. Complete sets, 95¢ and up. Casseroles—round, square, oval—40¢ to $1.65. Pie Plates, 40¢ to 65¢. Utility Dishes, 50¢ to $1.00. Custard Cups, 5¢.

Here are a few delicious, low-cost dishes you can cook in Pyrex Ovenware. More ideas can be had from The Pyrex Test Kitchen, Dept. 5704, Corning, N. Y.

Delicious and So Easy! Brush haddock fillets with beaten egg and crumbs. Place in greased Pyrex Casserole. Season. Cover with milk. Bake covered.

Try This for Sunday Dinner. Bone a breast of lamb. Spread with dressing. Roll and tie. Season. Place in Pyrex Utility Dish, with small potatoes and onions. Bake.

The Southwest Suggests Tamale Pie. To chopped meat add tomatoes, chili powder, onion, green pepper. Place layer of cornmeal mush in greased dish, add meat mixture. Cover with mush, bake.

Individual Service. Into Pyrex Custard Cups place bits of codfish, mix with cream sauce, season. Cover with mashed potatoes, bake.

A Tasty Dish! Halibut with oyster stuffing. Rub halibut with salt. Stuff with dressing. Bake covered in Pyrex Casserole.

Accompaniments

COOKER
SET

In this chapter are accompaniments for various main dishes and desserts found elsewhere in this book. The Farmer's Wife often paired stews and casseroles with side dishes such as mashed potatoes and buttered noodles, and topped her desserts with whipped cream. You'll find recipes for ten such accompaniments on the pages that follow with each providing enough to feed a crowd.

❦ Garlic Bread

1 loaf crusty bread of your choice
4 to 6 tbsp. butter, softened
2 cloves garlic, mashed to a paste
salt to taste

Preheat the oven to 350°F. Cut the loaf of bread in half lengthwise and pull open. Mix together the butter, garlic, and salt to taste. Spread on both insides of the loaf of bread. Wrap in aluminum foil and place in oven. Allow to warm 15 to 20 minutes until hot through.

❧ Corn Bread

1 ¾ c. cornmeal
¼ c. sugar
3 tsp. baking powder
⅓ tsp. salt
1 c. milk
1 egg
2 tbsp. oil, plus extra for oiling the skillet

Preheat oven to 425°F. Oil the inside of an 8-inch cast-iron skillet and place in the oven to heat while you mix the batter. Combine the dry ingredients and add the wet, whisking until the egg is well incorporated. Pour into hot skillet and bake 15 to 20 minutes until cooked through.

PHOTO: PETER DANT STUDIOS

❧ Buttermilk Biscuits

4 c. flour
¾ tsp. salt
4 tsp. baking powder
1 tsp. baking soda
1½ tbsp. sugar
8 tbsp. unsalted butter, softened, plus extra for buttering cookie sheets
scant 1½ c. buttermilk

Preheat oven to 450°F. Butter cookie sheets. Mix dry ingredients
together. Using a hand mixer, beat the butter into the dry ingredients
until the batter resembles coarse meal. Add buttermilk and stir to
incorporate. Turn the dough out onto a floured board and knead until
the dough holds together. Roll out to ½-inch thickness and cut into
rounds with the top of a glass. Place on cookies sheets and bake 12 to
28 minutes until done.

❦ Buttered Noodles

2 lbs. wide egg noodles
salt
unsalted butter
Italian parsley, chopped, if desired

Fill a large stockpot with water, add plenty of salt (this will ensure that the noodles are salty enough when you serve them), cover, and bring to a boil over a high flame. Add the noodles and cook according to package directions until al dente, stirring occasionally to prevent the noodles from sticking. Drain in a colander and pour into a bowl. Stir in butter in small pieces, mixing well. Add more butter a little at a time until the noodles are lightly coated. Sprinkle chopped parsley over noodles, if desired.

❧ Green Salad

½ lb. mixed leaves of different varieties (i.e., Bibb lettuce, baby spinach, arugula)
4 tbsp. good-quality olive oil
1 tbsp. good-quality red wine or sherry vinegar
salt and pepper to taste

Gently wash the leaves, spin in a lettuce spinner, and wrap in a kitchen towel to remove all moisture. Meanwhile, mix up remaining ingredients in a bowl with a small whisk. Just before you are ready to serve the salad, rip leaves into a bowl and pour dressing over them, using only enough to lightly coat the leaves. Serve immediately or salad will wilt.

❦ Buttered Peas

2 14-oz. packages sweet petite peas
1 tsp. salt
2 tbsp. unsalted butter
fresh mint leaves, chopped, if desired

Bring a large pot of water to boil over a high flame and add salt. Pour in peas and cook until just hot. Drain in a colander and pour peas into a bowl. Add butter and stir. Top with mint leaves, if desired.

❦ Slow Cooker Gravy

1 c. meat liquid from slow cooker
¼ c. white wine
2 sprigs fresh herbs, such as rosemary or thyme
2 tbsp. unsalted butter, slightly softened
2 tbsp. flour
salt and pepper to taste

After removing cooked meat from slow cooker, pour liquid into a large stockpot along with wine and herbs. Bring to a boil, then turn down flame to achieve a consistent simmer. With your fingers, on a small plate, mash together butter and flour to make small balls. Drop them one at a time into the simmering gravy and whisk until they are incorporated. Add one at a time until the gravy has achieved the desired thickness. Remove from flame, discard herbs, and taste for seasoning. Pour into a gravy boat or small pitcher to serve.

Perfect Whipped Cream

2 c. heavy whipping cream
3 tbsp. confectioner's sugar
2 tsp. vanilla

Using a large, chilled, stainless-steel bowl, whip the cream with a hand mixer until it begins to foam. Sprinkle in sugar and pour in vanilla. Continue to mix on high speed until soft peaks form. Serve immediately.

Resources

In compiling this book and testing the recipes, I relied on these four excellent volumes to guide me. At the time of this writing, not many cookbooks existed that gave recipes for wholesome, elegant, slow-cooked meals. The cookbooks written by Lynn Alley and Beth Hensperger and Julie Kaufmann go a long way toward rethinking what is possible and really should be possible (or completely avoided) in the slow cooker. They were instrumental in helping me conceive the best possible ways to convert *The Farmer's Wife*'s stove- and oven-cooked meals for the slow cooker. As for the work of the late, great food historian Alan Davidson, it is unlike the work of any other—thoughtful, comprehensive, and above all, funny. Anyone even marginally interested in the history of food should seek out his book.

How soup stock in your
FRIGIDAIRE
helps you build
many grand meals

Alley, Lynn. *The Gourmet Slow Cooker, Volumes I and II.* Berkeley, CA: Ten Speed Press, 2003, 2006.

Beth, and Julie Kaufmann. *Not Your Mother's Slow Cooker Cookbook.* Hensperger, Boston: The Harvard Common Press, 2005.

Davidson, Alan. *The Penguin Companion to Food.* New York: Penguin Books, 2002.

Kate Smith swaps stories
with Mrs. Dinsman of Burbank, Calif.

"TWO YEARS AGO I married an aircraft executive," writes Mrs. Joseph Dinsman of California. "My husband's position called for quite a bit of entertaining, and he was always proud when guests commented on my light cakes, biscuits, etc.

"Soon after we were married, my mother-in-law came to visit us. I guess she thought I couldn't cook, for she gave me all sorts of advice. One piece of advice was—if I'd use Calumet Baking Powder I'd always have good luck in baking.

"Imagine her surprise when I told her *four* generations of my family had used Calumet!"

CALUMET OLD-TIMERS CLUB

"MRS. DINSMAN, we ought to start a club," Kate answers, "—a *Calumet Old-Timer Club*. Because every day I hear from folks whose families have been using Calumet for generations.

"And there's only *one* reason for that. Dependability! Because Calumet's the 'Double-Acting' Baking Powder. Works once in the mixing bowl and again in the oven. Protects your baking *all the way!*

"I'm sending along a recipe for some holiday sugar cookies, a good wartime recipe low in fat and sugar!"

PARTY SUGAR COOKIES

2 cups sifted Swans Down Cake Flour	½ teaspoon salt	⅓ cup shortening
	½ teaspoon cinnamon	3 tablespoons milk
1 teaspoon Calumet Baking Powder	¼ teaspoon nutmeg	2 egg yolks, unbeaten
	⅔ cup sugar	½ teaspoon lemon extract

● Sift flour once, measure, add baking powder, salt, and spices, and sift again. Measure sugar into bowl. Heat shortening with milk until all shortening is melted. Add immediately to sugar and beat ½ minute. Add egg yolks; beat ½ minute longer. Add lemon extract and half of flour mixture and beat until blended. Then add remaining flour, ⅓ at a time, beating until smooth. Cover with waxed paper and chill several hours, or until firm enough to roll.

Roll dough ⅛ inch thick on lightly floured board. Cut with floured cutters in assorted shapes. Place on lightly greased baking sheet; sprinkle with sugar. Bake in hot oven (400° F.) 7 minutes, or until done. Makes about 2½ dozen cookies.

(All measurements are level.)

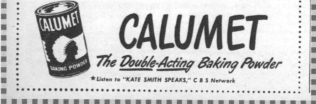

CALUMET
The Double-Acting Baking Powder

★ Listen to "KATE SMITH SPEAKS," C B S Network

Index

Adouba, 82
American Chop Suey, 68, 69
apples, 152
   Brown Betty, 154, 155
   Caramel Raisin Apple, 179
   Roast Pork and Apples, 75, 76
apricots, Rice and Apricot
   Pudding, 162
Asparagus Soup, 41
Banana Pudding, 169
"Barbecued" Beef on Toasted sBuns,
   89, 90
"Barbecued" Ribs, 90, 91
beanpot, 11, 12
beans, 58, 59, 60
   American Chop Suey, 68, 69
   Black Bean Soup, 34
   Boston Baked Beans, 11, 111
   Limas and Lamb Stew, 94, 95
   Succotash, 125
   Vegetable Stew, 66, 67
   Vegetable Stew, 66, 67
beef
   "Barbecued" Beef on Toasted

Buns, 89, 90
"Barbecued" Ribs, 90, 91
Beef Stew with Carrots, 47
Chili con Carne, 56, 57
Ground Steak, Italian Style,
   86, 87
Pot Roast, 100
Real Italian Spaghetti, 88
sauces, 103
Swedish Meatballs, 85
Tamale Pie Dinner, 62, 63
Boston Bakes Beans, 111
bread
   Corn Bread, 185
   Garlic Bread, 182
Brown Betty, 154, 155
Buttered Noodles, 189
Buttered Peas, 192
Buttermilk Biscuits, 188

cabbage
   Cabbage with Bacon, 127, 128
   Cabbage with Celery Seeds,
   127, 128

Cabbage with Chestnuts, 127, 128
Vegetable Stew, 66, 67
cake, English Gingerbread Cake, 172, 173
Calabasita y Gallina (Pumpkin and Chicken), 92, 93
Candied Orange Sweet Potatoes, 114, 115
Caper Sauce, 107
Caramel Bread Pudding, 148
Caramel Raisin Apple, 179
carrots
Beef Stew with Carrots, 47
Cream of Carrot Soup, 37
Normandy Carrots, 136
Vegetable Soup, 28, 29
Vegetable Stew, 66, 67
Casserole de Boeuf, 50
Casserole of Fowl, 49, 50
cauliflower
Cauliflower Cream Soup, 40
Cauliflower in Tomato Sauce, 122
celery
American Chop Suey, 68, 69
Cabbage with Celery Seeds, 127, 128
Cream of Celery Soup, 36
Vegetable Soup, 28, 29
Vegetable Stew, 66, 67
chestnuts, Cabbage with Chestnuts, 127, 128
chicken
Brunswick Stew, 54
Calabasita y Gallina (Pumpkin and Chicken), 92, 93
Casserole of Fowl, 49, 50

Chicken Curry, 79
Chicken with Dumplings, 50
Chili con Carne, 56–59
Clam Chowder, 42, 43
Coconut Bread Pudding, 142, 143
corn
Corn Bread, 185
Corn Chowder, 32
Corn Pudding, 133
Spoon Corn Bread, 131
Succotash, 125
cranberries
Cranberry Pudding, 175, 176
Spiced Cranberries, 138
cream, Perfect Whipped Cream, 196
Crème de Menthe Pears, 178
Creole Sauce, 104
Crock-Pot, 12, 13, 15
Currant Sauce, 106
dumplings, 50
eggplant, Escalloped Eggplant with Tomatoes and Onions, 121
English Gingerbread Cake, 172, 173
Escalloped Eggplant with Tomatoes and Onions, 121
Fig Rice Pudding, 165
fish, Down East Fish Chowder, 43
fowl, Casserole of Fowl, 49, 50
Garlic Bread, 182
Graham Pudding, 170
Green Salad, 190
gravy, Slow Cooker Gravy, 194
ham, Delicious Ham Dishes, 98
Horseradish Sauce, 104
Indian Pudding, 157
lamb

Lamb Curry, 77–79
Limas and Lamb Stew, 94, 95
Ragout of Lamb and Early
    Vegetables, 95
sauces, 103
Lemon Rice Pudding, 161
Lentil Stew, 63
Maître D'Hotel Butter, 107
Mexican Kidney Beans, 60
Mint Sauce, 106
mushrooms, American Chop Suey,
    68, 69
noodles, Buttered Noodles, 189
Normandy Carrots, 136
okra, Vegetable Stew, 66, 67
onions, Escalloped Eggplant with
    Tomatoes and Onions, 121
pears
    Crème de Menthe Pears, 178
    Poached Pears, 178
peas
    Buttered Peas, 192
    Green Pea Pudding, 135
    Split Pea Soup, 23, 24
    Vegetable Stew, 66, 67
Pennsylvania Rice Pudding, 166
Perfect Whipped Cream, 196
Plain Bread Pudding, 147
Poached Pears, 178
pork
    Adouba, 82
    American Chop Suey, 68, 69
    Pork Roast, 105
    Roast Pork and Apples, 75, 76
    sauces, 103
    Swedish Meatballs, 85

Pot Roast, 100
potatoes
    Cream of Potato Soup/Potato
    Chowder, 30
    Candied Orange Sweet Potatoes,
    114, 115
    Vegetable Soup, 28, 29
    Vegetable Stew, 66, 67
prunes
    Prune Bread Pudding, 154
    Prune Betty, 155
pudding
    Banana Pudding, 169
    Caramel Bread Pudding, 148
    Coconut Bread Pudding, 142, 143
    Corn Pudding, 133
    Cranberry Pudding, 175, 176
    Fig Rice Pudding, 165
    Graham Pudding, 170
    Green Pea Pudding, 135
    Indian Pudding, 157
    Lemon Rice Pudding, 161
    Pennsylvania Rice Pudding, 166
    Plain Bread Pudding, 147
    Prune Bread Pudding, 154
    Raisin and Chocolate Bread
    Pudding, 150
    Rice and Apricot Pudding, 162
    Rice Pudding with Dates, 166
Pumpkin, Calabasita y Gallina
    (Pumpkin and Chicken), 92, 93
Rabbit Curry, 79
Ragout of Lamb and Early
    Vegetables, 95
Raisin and Chocolate Bread
    Pudding, 150

Real Italian Spaghetti, 88
rhubarb, Stewed Rhubarb, 157
rice
   Fig Rice Pudding, 165
   Pennsylvania Rice Pudding, 166
   Rice and Apricot Pudding, 162
   Rice Pudding with Dates, 166
salad, Green Salad, 190
sauces, 103
   Caper Sauce, 107
   Creole Sauce, 104
   Currant Sauce, 106
   Horseradish Sauce, 104
   Maître D'Hotel Butter, 107
   Mint Sauce, 106
   Tomato Sauce, 70
Scalloped Tomatoes, 117, 119
Sheep's Head Stock and Soup, 20
Slow Cooker Gravy, 194
soups
   Asparagus Soup, 41
   Black Bean Soup, 34
   Cauliflower Cream Soup, 40
   Clam Chowder, 42, 43
   Corn Chowder, 32
   Cream of Carrot Soup, 37
   Cream of Celery Soup, 36
   Cream of Potato Soup/Potato
   Chowder, 30
   Cream of Spinach Soup, 38
   Down East Fish Chowder, 43
   Split Pea Soup, 23, 24
   Tomato Soup, 27, 28
   Vegetable Soup, 28, 29
Spaghetti, Real Italian Spaghetti, 88
Spiced Cranberries, 138

spinach
   Cream of Spinach Soup, 38
   Creamed Spinach, 38
Spoon Corn Bread, 131
stews
   Beef Stew with Carrots, 47
   Brunswick Stew, 54
   Lentil Stew, 63
   Limas and Lamb Stew, 94, 95
   Vegetable Stew, 66, 67
Stewed Rhubarb, 157
Succotash, 125
Swedish Meatballs, 85
Tamale Pie, 60
Tamale Pie Dinner, 62, 63
tomatoes
   Cauliflower in Tomato Sauce, 122
   Escalloped Eggplant with
   Tomatoes and Onions, 121
   Scalloped Tomatoes, 117, 119
   Tomato Sauce, 70
   Tomato Soup, 27, 28
   Vegetable Stew, 66, 67
Turkish Pilaf, 112
Veal Casserole, 96
Vegetable Soup, 28, 29
Vegetable Stew, 66, 67